Aurora

Dawn of a New Era

P&O Cruises

Text: Garry Pownall
Photography: Mike O'Dwyer
Concept, Design and Art Direction:
Theo Hodges Business Design Consultants

Aurora

Dawn of a New Era

The Peninsular and Oriental Steam Navigation Company

Contents

Foreword

Aurora. The Roman goddess of the dawn. What name could be more appropriate for the first ship to join the P&O Cruises fleet at the dawn of the new Millennium?

Aurora is a world-class contemporary superliner built for British passengers by P&O: the only company building new ships for the British cruise market. Her design incorporates some of the best innovative features to be found in any ship worldwide. The choice that she offers her passengers – from dining to entertainment and accommodation – is more extensive than that on any other British cruise ship.

Aurora's arrival brings to four the number of ships in P&O Cruises' British-based fleet. Each ship has her own character, distilled from the design of the vessel herself, the professionalism and warmth of those who man her and the standards set by the company for which she sails.

To these must be added the enthusiasm and affection of her passengers who, one hopes, will return again and again. In the years ahead, *Aurora* will carry thousands of passengers across the world and we are confident that, for them, she will become a stylish and exciting new home.

Aurora builds upon over 160 years of maritime experience and tradition within P&O. As the Group embarks on a new phase in its story with the creation of a separate cruise company, *Aurora* looks set to make her own chapter in history.

The Lord Sterling of Plaistow CBE
Chairman, The Peninsular and Oriental Steam Navigation Company

Right: a digital vision of *Aurora* off the island of Elba

AURORA
P&O

Behind t

ne Scenes

P&O Past

Inspired by traditional Moorish designs, these tiles by Russell Coates in *Aurora*'s Medina Restaurant are evocative of P&O's early links with Spain and Portugal

Above and opposite page: John Newberry's murals of Cairo and the Pyramids remind diners in *Aurora*'s Alexandria Restaurant of the Overland Route on the way to India

The red and white, blue and yellow flag flown from *Aurora*'s mast tells the world that she is a P&O ship. The handsome P&O house flag has been worn by about 1,200 ships since it was first hoisted at the beginning of Queen Victoria's reign and its colours hint at how this great shipping line began. For these are the heraldic colours of the royal families of Spain and Portugal.

Aurora's earliest predecessors sailed every week to the Iberian peninsular, carrying passengers, goods and mail. Sea-going steam ships were very novel in 1837. They were powered by single cylinder engines of huge bore (often the piston was six or seven feet in diameter). They huffed and puffed, clanked and shuddered, turning the splashing paddle wheels at about 16 revolutions per minute, using great quantities of coal and often breaking down. Wisely, they carried a full suit of sails too, but unlike sailing ships, they could put to sea whatever the wind. And that was why despite all the problems, steam ships were the way of the future: they offered a certainty which shipping had never known before. No longer having to wait for the right wind meant regular mails, a competitive cargo business and a predictable relaxing routine for passengers.

In 1840, the line shaped its course for the east and began to run a regular service through the Mediterranean to Egypt and beyond. In those days, a letter to India took three months to deliver by the fastest land and sea route. Passengers, who usually preferred to sail via Cape Town, had to allow five or six months at sea. P&O's directors knew that good steam-

ers properly managed could offer a far better service and they set about providing it.

The difficulties they overcame would make a modern travel agent shudder. Before the Suez Canal opened in 1869, all P&O's passengers to India were taken from Alexandria to the Red Sea overland. These were not small parties; in 1857, a total of 8,293 P&O passengers travelled this way. They stayed the night in Cairo and set off across the desert to Suez, six at a time, in two-wheeled horse-drawn buses. The journey usually took 18 hours, and sometimes the buses got lost. Each first-class passenger was allowed one camel-load of baggage without surcharge. Other camels plodded along with the hundreds of wooden boxes containing the Royal Mail. And most astonishingly, because sailing colliers could not easily make their way up the Red Sea, P&O was obliged to carry all the coal its steamers needed at Suez across the desert, camel-load by camel-load.

Once the Suez Canal was open, P&O could get the mail and the passengers from London to Bombay in 16 days and it did, with astonishing reliability. The service to Australia was equally regular. Out of 468 arrivals in Melbourne over three years in the 1880s, only seven were more than 60 minutes late, despite voyages halfway round the world.

P&O was quick, but by modern standards the passenger facilities on Victorian ships were very simple. Ventilation was a matter of rigging a sail over the companionways when the heat became insupportable. The perennial myth that 'posh' meant having a shady cabin on the Port side Out and Starboard Home would have amused the Victorians, for the entire ship sweltered from the Gulf of Suez to the Arabian Sea. Men bathed on deck; women managed below with basins of tepid water.

The motion of the ship if the sea was rough could be very uncomfortable, but at the time P&O ships were thought to be wonderfully steady and safe. The *Himalaya* of 1854, then the largest and most powerful vessel in the world, pitched and rolled so violently crossing the Bay of Biscay in quite ordinary weather on her maiden voyage that many passengers stayed up all night in fear and a jib-boom crashed down the fore cabin stairs. It was to be another hundred years before dynamic stabilizers calmed the roughest seas and P&O passengers slept soundly. Candles and lamps were always extinguished (for safety reasons) at 10pm and you went to bed, like it or not.

And yet the Victorians went to sea for pleasure too. As long ago as 1844 P&O offered round trips on the smaller ships which worked the branches off its main line through the Mediterranean. Shore excursions were made from ports such as Athens and Jaffa (for the Holy Land); previously inaccessible places of enormous interest to a public which had been brought up on churchgoing, Latin and Greek. Invalids sailed to Madeira or the healthy Norwegian fjords. P&O, which converted its oldest liner into the 'cruising yacht' *Vectis* in 1904, took full advantage of the new holiday concept.

By the 1920s, larger and grander ships added comfort to the traditional P&O virtues of service and reliability. All *Viceroy of India*'s first-class passengers had single berth cabins with hot and cold running water (second-class still only had cold). She was very fast and her turbo-electric engines made her as silent and free from vibration as *Aurora*. But the point of the *Viceroy* (launched in 1929) was her extraordinary interior. There were Scottish broadswords on the panelled walls of the 'baronial' smoking room, mock Chippendale furniture in the Adam-style reading room, and P&O's first enclosed pool.

Canberra, designed in 1957, changed the way P&O ships looked from the shore. Her funnels and machinery were placed aft to make more space for passengers. For ten years she was the supreme liner to Australia and then she was adapted as a one-class ship for cruising, for by the 1970s, jet aircraft had taken over the ocean liners' trade.

An era was over, but 140 years' experience of building and managing superb ships was not wasted. P&O still flies the same flag on the finest passenger ships afloat. They offer a cruising experience very unlike the P&O liners of old: more sophisticated, more contemporary and more tailored to the individual. The lights stay on after 10pm – and shore excursions *never* get lost in the desert.

Design and Build

One wet and blustery day in December 1998, about 150 people met at a small town near the borders of Holland and Germany. Papenburg (35,000 inhabitants) is surrounded by immense, neatly harrowed fields which stretch flat and dull to the horizon; vegetables or tulip bulbs would seem to be Papenburg's business. But here it was, 45 km from the sea, that *Aurora* was to be built and the guests of the Meyer Werft (shipyard) had come to see her keel laid. The Peninsular and Oriental Steam Navigation Company is long-established, but Joseph L. Meyer GmbH is older. This family firm has been building ships at Papenburg since 1795 and in that time has sent about 700 vessels down the River Ems to the North Sea.

Vast building dock

The ceremony took place in Meyer's covered building dock. Imagine a concrete swimming pool 358 metres (1,174 ft.) long and 39 metres (128 ft.) wide set in an immense factory shed. Near one end, a moveable dam had been fitted, beyond which a ship for an Asian company was being finished. Straddling the dock is a gantry crane capable of lifting 600 tonnes. It easily picked up the first prefabricated section of *Aurora*'s hull, a rusty-red chunk the size of a row of terraced houses, and laid it gently on the dock floor. The band played, some *gluwein* was drunk and then the welders went to work again. A ship had to be built and there was little over a year to do it in.

Until Summer 1999, more and more such blocks, which had been built in the assembly shop next to the dock (or in yards down river), were lifted into place and welded to one another. By 7th August there was a recognisable ship sitting on the floor of the dock and on that day the dam was removed (the other ship had sailed in the spring), the dock was flooded and *Aurora* floated for the first time in her life. Then, just a week into the New Millennium, the propellers were fitted and cautious tugs nudged *Aurora* (still known by the yard as Ship 640) out into the River Ems. Her funnel, too tall for the covered dock, was craned on board and the final stages of fitting-out began.

Four design teams

Watching the keel-laying that winter day were members of the four design teams working with P&O and Meyer Werft, the men and women who translate P&O's ideas for a new ship into drawings the yard can work from. Anders Johanssen was there, representing the distinguished Swedish marine architect Robert Tillberg who coordinated the whole design effort. The Norwegian Petter Yran and Alison Clixby from London were there; John McNeece could not be. Each design team had a great deal left to do. But at last the designers could see the metal taking shape and they knew that a great ship was scarcely 12 months away – a ship which they already knew would be contemporary, British, stylish and very beautiful.

JOS.L.MEYER PAPENBURG
PAPENBURG

The Ship's Company

The mooring ropes are hauled in. The bandsmen on the quay thump and trill through *A Life On The Ocean Wave*, put their music away and go off for tea. The ship slips from her berth and your holiday at sea begins. But what of the men and women who live their lives on the ocean wave? When you sail on *Aurora*, 850 people sail with you to look after the ship and to make sure that you have a wonderful time. Who are they?

Engine Room

52 of them are in the Engine Department under the Chief Technical Officer, a powerful man indeed and the only officer apart from the Captain to live in a Special Suite. In Victorian times the grubby engineers were men apart, patronised by the deck officers. They struggled with primitive machinery and pressure from the company to economise with coal and yet to deliver speed and avoid breakdowns. *Aurora*'s 15 spotless Technical Officers (respected by all their shipmates) are British. Two are cadets who are gaining sea experience while being sponsored by P&O at college. They hope for the Special Suite one day and responsibility for all of a ship's machinery. Of the 34 Engine Ratings, most are from the Philippines. Some work in the engine rooms; others do jobs around the ship like welding, plumbing, turning wood or metal, painting and polishing. The carpenter, whose predecessors could repair a mast or even patch the hull, now tends to mend furniture.

Specialists

P&O ships at sea were completely out of touch with land until the advent of radio in 1908. Today the old Radio Officer's job is handled by the Electro-Technical Department whose nine British officers and five Filipino ratings are responsible for anything electrical, from radar to food mixers. Other specialists aboard include the two doctors in their red striped epaulettes (like RN surgeon officers) and four nurses; five photographers; eight croupiers from the casino; the 17 beauticians; the two printers, the port lecturer, the seamstress/upholsterer; the four Ghurka security patrolmen who guard the gangway in port, the three bandleaders, the solo pianist and the ballroom dancing instructor.

A Grand Hotel

The Executive Purser's job is similar to that of the General Manager of a grand hotel and his is called the Hotel Department, but this 'hotel' moves. Warned by a message (ending with the traditional "All Well" with which P&O ships at sea have always reassured their owners) the company's Agent will be on the quayside when *Aurora* docks, accompanied by the local officials needed to clear the passengers ashore. The Executive Purser is at the gangway to greet them with the ship's Bill of Health, Ammunition Declaration, lists of luxury goods, etc. And then the things he has ordered while at sea begin to arrive: British newspapers for the passengers in staterooms and suites; fresh flowers; sometimes extra fresh food if the local supplier is known and trusted.

Shopping for *Aurora*

The Executive Purser orders everything *Aurora* needs. His shopping list is long: 2,500 items, from furniture polish to figs, from dill to disposable nappies. There are 1,200 food items in the freezers, chill rooms and stores below and the ship carries enough for one extra cruise as a back-up. On world cruises she carries 90 days' worth and then he has to look to his stores of back bacon (not streaky, thank you), Stilton cheese, kippers and sausages that British passengers mind about.

The Executive Purser's 595 staff look after your cabin, prepare and serve everything you eat and drink, and from their offices behind the Reception Desk in the Atrium, smilingly solve what sometimes seems like a thousand problems a day. A passenger wants to move from the Medina to the Alexandria restaurant; difficult, but we will do what we can. The Librarian has vanished; I think it's his lunch break madam. The ship-to-shore phone doesn't seem to be working; have you remembered the international code, sir? So it goes on.

There are very few complaints because the ship is so well run, but those that there are must be entered in the Complaints Book. The Executive Purser reads it every morning, noting the action taken, asking for fuller reports if the matter sounds sufficiently important. The Complaints Book is taken very seriously indeed.

Two couples have wedding anniversaries tomorrow and on this cruise that entitles them to a champagne reception; warn the Captain (by e-mail), check with the photographers, advise the galley about the names on the cakes. How does she spell Leslie? Would it be possible to have a different kind of pillow? Can I give a private party on board? Can my travel agent reserve the same stateroom for me next year? Yes, yes, yes.

The Entertainments Department under the Cruise Director is large and important. Without it you, the passengers, would have to make your own fun as Victorian passengers did, but we will look at the entertainers separately and the work of the chefs and bar staff too.

Left: Brian Purnell, *Aurora*'s Executive Purser briefing his crew at the daily morning meeting. Above: staff in Reception solve problems with a smile

The Bridge

Captain Burgoine on the bridge

Seven decks above, the bridge is completely calm. The officers concentrate, though the atmosphere is as easy-going as you would expect among young men in their twenties. Most will qualify as First Officers before they are 30, with Master's Certificates of Competence which entitle them (in theory) to take over the ship. There are 11 Deck Officers, mostly British, as are the senior ratings, divided into three watches. The two Second Officers and two Third Officers are the primary watch-keepers, four hours on, eight off. On the quieter watch, between 12 to 4 in the afternoon, there are one or two fewer.

Steady as she goes

The bridge monitors everything. The officers meticulously note down times and temperatures, alterations of course, ships passed and messages received, like nurses in an intensive care ward. Gone are the clanging engine room telegraphs and voice tubes; gone is the coxswain standing at a varnished wooden wheel; gone is the brass binnacle. *Aurora* is automated and electronic.

The Captain is responsible in law for the safe conduct of the ship and his authority aboard is absolute. It was said of an earlier P&O commander that he ought to have been a bishop but was none the worse a captain for that. The Captain of *Aurora* can sound very like a bishop when he reads the morning service on Sundays, but if something displeases him at his daily conference with the heads of departments he may not. He has to be diplomat, managing director, father-figure, salesman, bon viveur and calm technician. Above all he has to be a supreme seaman.

Seamanship

If you watch the Captain turn *Aurora* in a crowded port, peering over the bridge wing while his officers murmur their estimates of the shrinking gap between the ship and the shore, quickly glancing at the flag on the bow to judge the strength of the crosswind, gently coaxing the vessel round with skilfully judged bursts of the thrusters, you will see both the boy playing with the world's best arcade game and a man with awesome responsibilities on his shoulders. The ship turns safely. The Captain smiles. It was for that moment that he joined P&O as a cadet 30 years ago.

Ocean Showboat

Behind the glamour and glitter of a show lie hours of painstaking practice. Right and opposite page: Phil Raymond, *Aurora*'s Cruise Director, oversees intensive rehearsals ashore

It is easy to laugh at the way they used to entertain the passengers in the past. Little was done during the day. Committees of bossy people got up egg-and-spoon races, tugs-of-war and skipping contests. The Purser provided cards, edifying books and some board games. And it was hardly more exciting in the evenings. Every P&O ship had a piano and some had harmoniums too. Many of the stewards doubled as bandsmen and played violins, cornets or clarinets for dancing. But most of the entertainment was provided by the passengers themselves.

Recitations and encores

The P&O archives in the National Maritime Museum at Greenwich keep many Victorian travellers' letters. They paint a grim picture. "On Tuesday evening a grand concert was given by the passengers of the Second Saloon. The night was warm, so the piano was taken on deck and awnings were arranged to make the best of the singing.... After a brief interval Mr Hosking sang *Simon the Cellerer* and encored the last verse. A recitation, *The Elf Child* by little Miss May Longmore was followed by *The Death of Nelson* by Mr Whittaker, who had to respond to an imperative encore and rendered *Tis but a Little Faded Flower*." This is not the sort of repertoire the modern Cruise Director is looking for.

Today, Cruise Directors bring show business to sea. It is true that the Cruise Director will also be responsible for organising the bridge competitions, the ship's daily newspaper, the line dancing and the quizzes. The Youth Crew report to him and so do the port lecturer, the ballroom dancing instructor and the classical musician. He supervises the work of nearly 80 people aboard whose job it is to make your cruise more entertaining. But at the heart of entertainment aboard *Aurora* are the shows.

West End quality

The Stadium Theatre Company is the P&O variety company, the singers and dancers who bring West End professionalism and excitement to the ships' theatres and show lounges. On *Canberra* in the 1960s, shows were produced on deck in an area called the Stadium. It was cramped and often impossibly hot, but show-business people are sentimental and the name stuck.

Aurora's Curzon Theatre is air-conditioned and equipped with the latest audio, lighting and scene-changing technology to give the shows the greatest impact. Every season, new performers are auditioned in London and rehearse intensively ashore so that when they join the ship every step, every note and every costume change are perfect – every night. For the biggest shows, extra dancers are brought in from the ship's regular cruise staff. But never again will a passenger be called upon to sing *Simon the Cellerer* or recite *The Elf Child*.

Art on Board

There are more pictures aboard *Aurora* - about 3,000 - than there are on the walls of the National Gallery in London. She is a very contemporary, very British ship and the artists whose work you enjoy on board are contemporary British artists.

A long tradition

Lord Sterling, P&O's Chairman, has always liked his ships to be travelling exhibitions of the best of British art. In this he takes after Sir Colin Anderson, also a connoisseur, whose Orient Line merged with P&O in 1960. Sir Colin commissioned works of art for the first *Oriana* from Graham Sutherland, Edward Bawden, John Piper, Ceri Richards and many others whose names were not as well known then as they are today. He established a tradition of taking fine art to sea.

To find the right artists for *Aurora* and to hand-hold them gently through conception, gestation and delivery (on time) P&O employed as midwife a genial art consultant, Tom Tempest-Radford. Tom's brief was to buy pictures which met three conditions. They had to flatter and enlarge the cabins and public spaces where they hung; there was to be nothing too disturbing, nothing gloomy. They had to bridge the gap between those who know about art and those who do not, pleasing both. And it was hoped that the exclusive *Aurora* collection would gain in value as earlier P&O works of art have done.

To this end, all the smaller works are prints actually pulled by the artists, not the photographic reproductions which hotels and lesser ships usually use. Every artist worked to precise dimensions on shipyard drawings of each bulkhead (the mariner's word for wall). The layout, the 'hang' as art experts say, of the pictures on the walls had to be as exact as the pictures on the pages of this book.

A floating gallery

The staircases provide the best spaces for large pieces and *Aurora*'s artists have made the most of them. Important new paintings by Nick Hely-Hutchinson, Lizzie Riches and Ginette Lassen light up the stairways where previous ships only had plain panels. And their strongly individual paintings will make it easier for passengers to remember which stair they are climbing or descending.

Right: John Mills at work on the Atrium sculpture shown above

The biggest work of art aboard is John Mill's water-carrier which stands 35 feet high in the Atrium. Deliberately reminiscent of the work of René Lalique, whose moulded glass was enormously influential in the 1930s, John's work was modelled in white polystyrene, before being cast in greeny-blue translucent resin.

Left: a painting by Nick Hely-Hutchinson for one of *Aurora*'s stairways

Food and Drink

Executive Chef of *Aurora* Haydn Davis, in his galley

The galley under construction at Meyer Werft

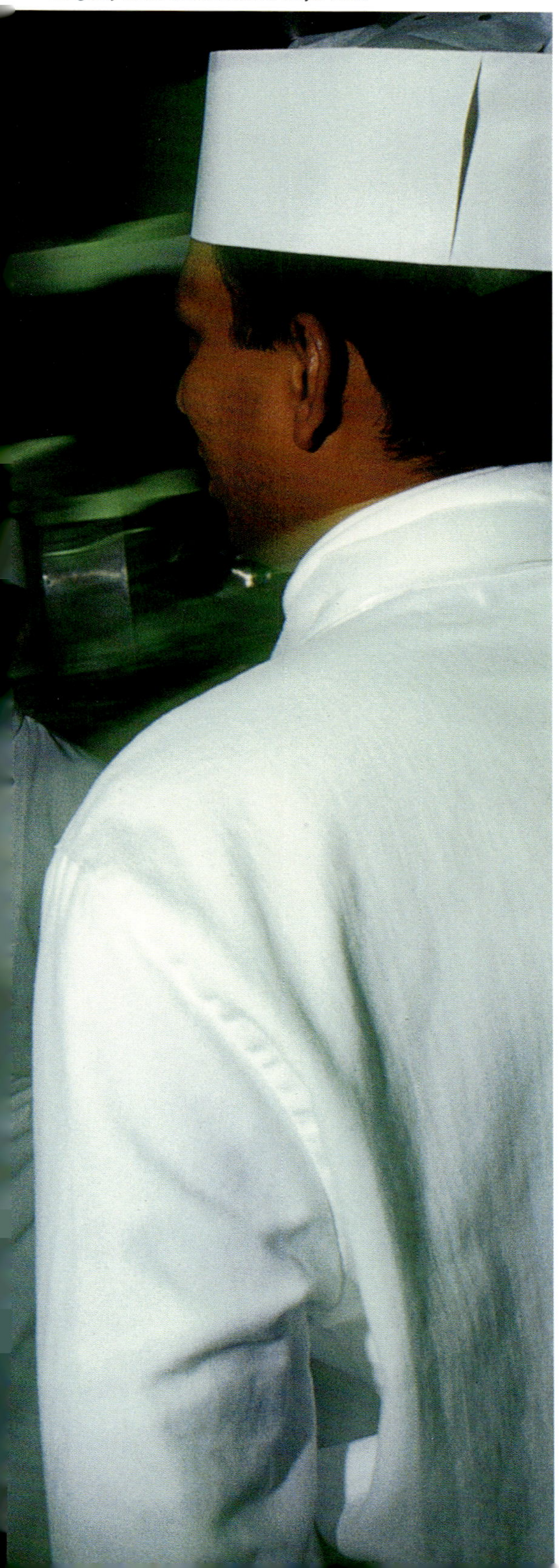

Aurora's main galley is rather larger than your kitchen. It needs to be, for in it are cooked most of the 116,500 main meals served during a typical two-week cruise. In fact it measures 32 metres (105 ft.) in each direction. On the deck below is the crew galley and on two still lower decks, the enormous larders, chill rooms and stores in which the Executive Purser and Executive Chef have laid up the provisions for your voyage. There are dry stores and dairy stores, vegetable stores and fruit stores, special rooms for red and white meat, poultry and fish; all kept at exactly the right temperatures for hygiene and flavour.

Freshness and safety

Cheese is kept at 4°C; root vegetables and potatoes at 5°C; fresh fruit and salad at 3°C; soft fruit slightly warmer, at 7°C; fat and butter, frozen fish, meat and poultry are all chilled to -25°C. There are special rooms in which frozen food is thawed, in which fish and vegetables are prepared and, of course, in which the washing-up is done. There is an ice carving room, a room for the cooking oil and even a special room for the bone crusher.

In these store rooms are vast quantities of food. On an average 14-day cruise, *Aurora*'s passengers and crew will eat 15 tons of meat, 4 tons of fish, 7 tons of poultry and game, 3½ tons of bacon, ham and gammon, and 28 tons of fresh fruit and vegetables. Butter, fats and cheese, 4½ tons. Ice cream, 4,000 litres. 51,000 eggs will go, as will 42,000 afternoon cakes and pastries. The bread consumption seems quite modest by comparison at 70,000 rolls and 3,600 loaves. And all this is eaten in two weeks. The ship stores twice the quantity it needs, just in case.

Of drink there is plenty too. Out of the wine and spirit stores come nearly 8,000 bottles of wine in a fortnight, 200 gallons of draught beer and 62,500 cans of ale, stout and lager. 3,000 bottles of mineral water and 10,000 cans of fruit juice assuage the thirst of more temperate passengers and the many Muslim members of the crew.

Free drinks

In the past, drinks were completely free of charge on P&O ships but this golden era was brought to an end in 1871 by the combined pressure applied on the company by the Total Abstinence societies and those who thought that the fares were too high. On Sundays and Thursdays the line provided champagne. On other days of the week beers, claret, sherry, rum, brandy, port, gin and whisky (in that order of popularity) flowed freely. Passengers were even given a glass of sherry when they booked their passages at the P&O offices.

In mid-Victorian times, lunch at sea consisted only of biscuits and cheese, but the breakfast with which passengers started the day was substantial; mutton chops, kedgeree (named after a town the ships passed on the way into Calcutta), eggs, and bacon, washed down with plenty of India Pale Ale and spirits. Dinner was the meal which counted. It usually began at four or five in the afternoon. From the menus which have survived we know that the Victorians ate prodigiously. However hot the weather, there was always mutton broth and boiled fowls, roast beef, roast veal, duck, goose, compote of pigeon, stewed ox tongue, cold meats galore and then every kind of stodgy and fattening pudding. Your menu on any P&O liner today will be totally different. There is plenty, certainly, but the emphasis is on stylish dishes, healthy eating and choice. And alas, you are now charged for drinks.

Ports of Call

Above: Geirangerfjord, Norway
Left: a launch returns passengers from St Peter Port, Guernsey

Left: Venice

Early in the morning, 692 times this year, a P&O Cruises ship will arrive at another anchorage or port. Every such destination is eagerly anticipated by the passengers. You peep through your cabin curtains. There it is! This is one of the reasons you came on a cruise. Get up! Go ashore! This is the way to travel!

Some cruise lines always go to the same ports; every other Tuesday they are in Cannes, every other Thursday in Barcelona, 16 times a year between May and October. Track itineraries make life easy for the operations staff who make one booking for 16 calls to the same berth (at a special discount) and for the coach operators who will be there too.

The P&O difference

P&O Cruises does it differently. From about 700 possible destinations the planners work out an itinerary for each ship which must meet three criteria. The programme must look good in the brochure; the ports must deliver on their promises; and the whole package must be practicable. It sounds easy. Actually it makes Rubik's Cube seem like noughts and crosses.

To design a cruise that looks really attractive in the travel agent's office, the planners put as many ports of call as they can into the voyage. It is not a cynical exercise; passengers want to visit as many places as possible during their holiday, though some find that once in the comfort of the ship their appetite for shore excursions diminishes. Humankind is slow to learn and the cruise brochure, like a menu, reflects the fact that our appetites often exceed our capacities. The travel agent, like the maître d'hôtel, knows it.

Style matters

Then the style of each ship must be reflected in its destinations. *Aurora*'s itineraries will be a little more individual than her elder sisters', but the ports visited must offer an enjoyable experience. Some places sound marvellous (e.g. Port au Prince, 'distant Ophir') but simply are not. Perhaps there is not much to do ashore, or the harbour is too far from the attractions.

Out come the planners' calendars. Two trans-Atlantic cruises are added to the plan. Fly-cruising, though not central to the P&O philosophy, turns a long ocean run into a real vacation. Then the six weeks of school holidays are marked off for family-length cruises to family destinations in the sun. The programme is taking shape.

Distances count

The next test of a draft cruise is whether it can be done. Starting from Southampton as almost all P&O cruises do, for there is no more convenient starting-point for most passengers, one must allow nearly three days' run to the Mediterranean. *Aurora* is designed to operate at 24 knots (nearly 28 m.p.h.) and will do so in all but the heaviest end-of-season weather, when the Captain may ease back a little to make the ship feel and sound more comfortable. She can only sail some 575 nautical miles in 24 hours and a ten-hour port call reduces the daily trip to about 330 nautical miles, so the mathematics of the chart table impose their own logic on the possible itinerary.

There are some interesting towns on the run south and the marketing department wants as many ports and as many different countries visited as possible to add precious variety to the programme. Vigo is perfectly placed for a stop on the way to Gibraltar; La Coruña for the journey back from Palma. But unfortunate Oporto is either just too near or just too far. A stop there means losing a more attractive call further south. The distance between ports begins to assume great importance.

Where will they put the inevitable Sunday call? Livorno is no good because the shops in nearby Florence will be closed. And she cannot go to Civitavecchia (for Rome) on Monday because the Sistine Chapel closes on Mondays. Better go to a resort like Cannes where the shopkeepers never rest. P&O's operations people know that kind of detail about the 334 possible ports of call and write the port guides to every one to make your visit more enjoyable. When you cruise with P&O your holiday is the product of incomparable expertise. The company which invented deep sea cruising has been perfecting it ever since.

The Blue Mosque, Istanbul

Around the World

It's a Friday in January. It gets dark before teatime. Christmas is over. There are a lot of colds about. The roads are treacherous and the dockside in Southampton will be chilly. But some of the luckiest people on earth can ignore all that. *Aurora* is about to leave on her World Cruise and the passengers settling into their cabins can look forward to 90 days of sunshine, luxury and enjoyment. They are not just off on a cruise, they are embarking on an epic travel adventure. They are about to sail around the world in the finest, most stylish ship P&O has ever built.

Once in a lifetime

Everyone has a place which they would like to visit once in a lifetime, an idea they roll around in their imaginations and keep returning to. Perhaps they dream of standing on the Mount of Olives looking (as so many have dreamed of doing) across at Jerusalem. Perhaps they are drawn towards the tranquil gardens of Japan; or they will want to board the bullet train which can whirl them in 26 minutes from Yokohama (where *Aurora* lies) to Tokyo's teeming shops. Shanghai or Singapore draw people who are fascinated by the Chinese way of life and would like to see something of it for themselves.

Many busy people daydream of restful pleasures on the beaches of Barbados, Antigua or Phuket. Wriggle your toes and you can almost feel the hot white sand, imagine the cool glass in your hand. Look, there is *Aurora*, admired by all who see her anchored in the bay, white on blue, your stylish home right around the world. Try it.

Sydney and Hong Kong are dream-inspiring places too; the trip on the Star Ferry across to the Peak, sunset falling on the Opera House, once enjoyed they will never be forgotten. And all these dreams come true on *Aurora*'s World Cruise.

A great British tradition

Between January and the beginning of April, *Aurora* will call at 27 ports from which her passengers can visit some of the most wonderful places the world can show a traveller. She will sail 34,182 nautical miles. She will transit the two most famous and dramatic canals in the world. And she will carry her passengers across three great oceans and the loveliest seas to visit five continents – safely, comfortably and in the uniquely British style that P&O has been perfecting since Victorian times.

Clockwise from left: Hong Kong; palm trees at Bottom Bay, Barbados; Golden Gate Bridge, San Francisco; the Opera House, Sydney

P&O Today

When in port, the host country's flag flies with the P&O flag

A proud tradition

Hanging on the wall of the boardroom in P&O's elegant headquarters building in Pall Mall the privileged visitor may see a magnificent document. Along the top are engraved images of Britannia, of tall ships and of blindfold Impartial Justice with her scales. Down the sides, the English lion, Irish harp and Scottish thistle may be found half hidden in the kind of swirling bosky foliage that used to adorn old banknotes. Beneath, on a red silk thread, hangs a golden seal, cracked with age it must be said, but still clearly depicting a queen enthroned. And over it all, a jaunty royal coat of arms and the headline in the calligrapher's largest hand – Victoria by the Grace of God, etc. – and the 21-year-old queen herself, framed in the elaborate whorls of the lettering. The Peninsular and Oriental Steam Navigation Company has never been a Limited Company as lesser shipping companies have been, nor is it a plc (public limited company). It is incorporated by Royal Charter dated 1840.

What could be more British? What is remarkable is that the modern company, while still rather grand and still treasuring its royal connections, while still overtly patriotic, proud to send its ships to the South Atlantic to help recover the Falklands and preferring its British-based ships to fly the Red Ensign, has constantly reinvented itself, vigorously adapting its corporate experience and skill to new markets in Europe, America and the Far East. This talent for reinvention has resulted in the planned 'demerger' of the cruise business to create a separate P&O company.

A wealth of expertise

In recent times the group diversified away from the sea and acquired Earls Court and Olympia, Bovis the construction company, Chelsea Harbour and holiday resorts in Australia. It even owned catering and joinery companies. Today P&O concentrates on three types of maritime business; cruises, ferries and ports. The group operates 171 ships and port facilities from New York to the Phillipines. These are very profitable growing industries with obvious synergies and are clearly recognisable as the kind of business P&O does best. Of the three, cruises is the largest and fastest-growing.

P&O Cruises is the part of the company most of *Aurora*'s passengers know best but the largest part of P&O cruise operations is Princess Cruises, based in Los Angeles and primarily operating to the Caribbean, Alaska and Europe. Princess operates 10 ships with a total capacity of 16,600 berths. Its 109,000 ton *Grand Princess*, launched in 1998, is the second largest cruise liner ever built. Like her sister ships, her deck officers are generally British, her staff Italian. She has established the concept of Grand Class Cruising in America, offering passengers more choice and less formality, and has been fully booked since she was built. When the present clutch of new-builds (as shipping companies call ships under construction) go into service, total capacity of Princess Cruises will double. In other words, 30,000 Americans will be at sea with P&O at any one time. To make such an impression on the US market is a remarkable achievement for a 'very British' company.

The specialists

There are niche cruise markets served by P&O too. Swan Hellenic operates chartered ships and the specially built *Minerva* on its highly individual discovery cruises, both at sea and on rivers such as the Nile (where P&O took the overland passengers to India in the 1840s). And a move has been made for the first time to serve continental European markets with the acquisition by P&O of *Aida*, the largest ship in the German market, and other German cruise businesses.

But *Aurora* has been built specifically for the British market. P&O Cruises, whose other ships (*Oriana*, *Arcadia* and *Victoria*) offer British cruise passengers a modern cruising experience like no other – stylish, welcoming, sophisticated, and so professionally managed that few would ever dream of sailing with another line – intends to make *Aurora* the most charismatic liner on the seven seas. Who doubts that they will succeed?

Oriana, launched in 1995, is *Aurora*'s elder sister, built in the same yard

All

Shipshape

Bulbous bow
Hidden beneath the water, under the ship's stem, is the bulbous bow which reduces the drag on the hull caused by the bow wave. The bulb is longer than two London buses and almost as high as they would be stacked one on top of the other.

Bow thrusters/stern thrusters
Three 1,500 kW electric motors power the bow thrusters beneath the waterline just aft of the bulbous bow, and a fourth powers the stern thruster between the propeller shafts. The thruster motors drive Lips controllable-pitch propellers placed in tunnels running across the centreline of the ship. They provide sideways thrust (in either direction) and make *Aurora* easily manoeuvrable in harbour without the help of tugs.

The Bridge
Totally enclosed to protect its delicate electronic equipment from the damp sea air, the bridge looks quite like the control room of a large TV studio. 29" video screens display information from the ship's radars, satellite navigation equipment and the chart data stored electronically in the ship's computers. *Aurora* is conned automatically most of the time, but when she is steered manually, the steersman uses a small multi-directional joystick.

Engines
Aurora is powered by four 14-cylinder MAN B&W diesel engines. Each one has a capacity of about 1,520 litres and weighs over 209 tonnes. The four engines deliver 79,860 horsepower, or 58,800 kW, which is converted to electricity. Some is used for the 'hotel' side of the ship (lights, air conditioning, cookers, etc.); most powers the two massive 20,000 kW electric motors which turn the propellers.

Stabilisers
Two metal wings – stabilisers – each 6.1 metres (20 ft.) long, stick out of each side of the hull, under the water. As the ship begins to roll over a wave – the normal sway of a ship which passengers find uncomfortable – the stabilisers twist to exert an opposite force in the water to keep *Aurora* steady. A computer, sensing the ship's movement, automatically provides the stream of instructions to the powerful hydraulic jacks which twist the 98 tonne 'wings' one way and another in the water.

Propellers
Swedish-made by a company in the Rolls-Royce group, the twin five-bladed propellers are 5.8 metres (19 ft.) in diameter. Because the output of her electric propulsion motors is so flexible, *Aurora*'s propellers can be the simple fixed-pitch type. (Pitch is the angle at which the blades slice into the water).

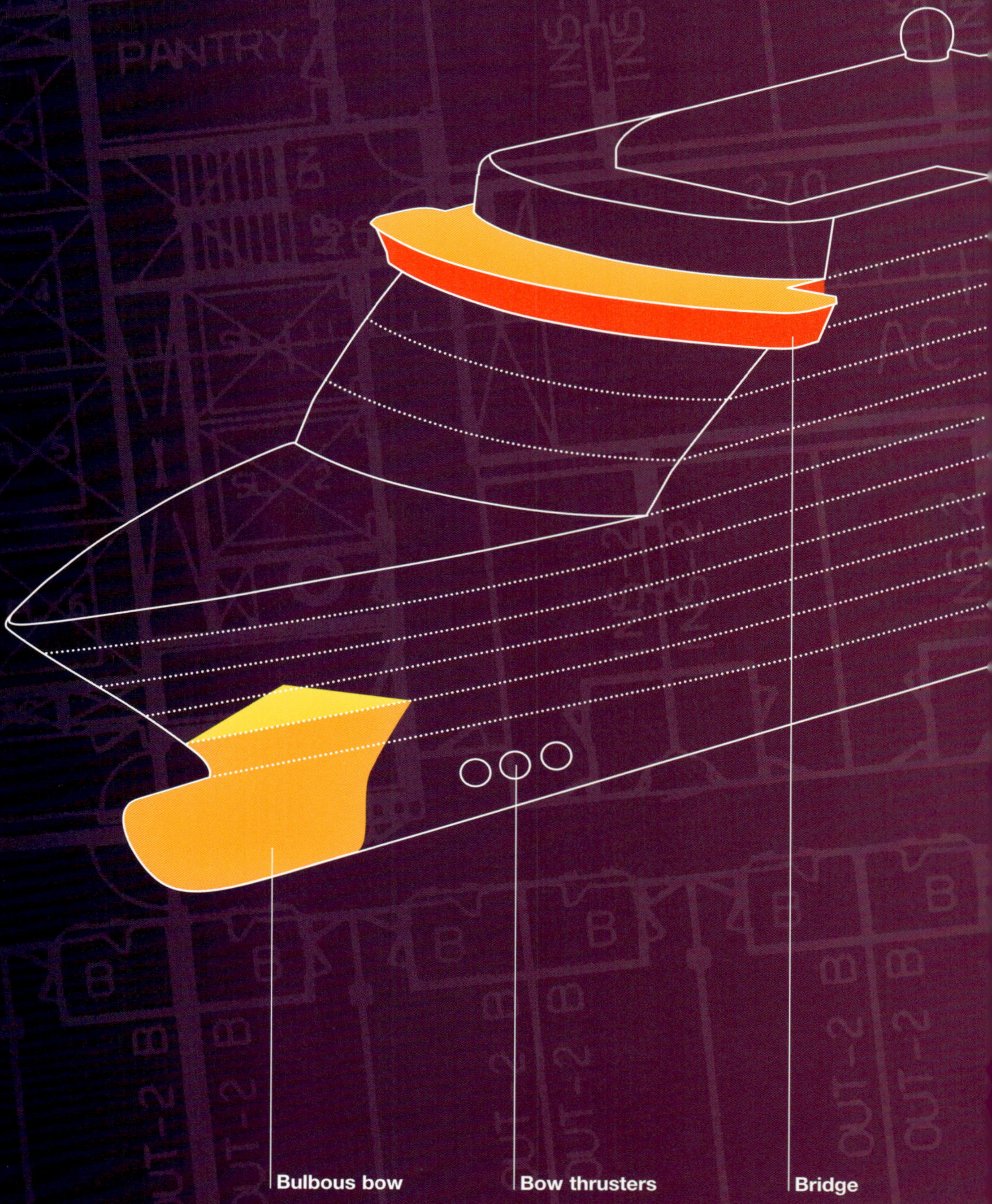

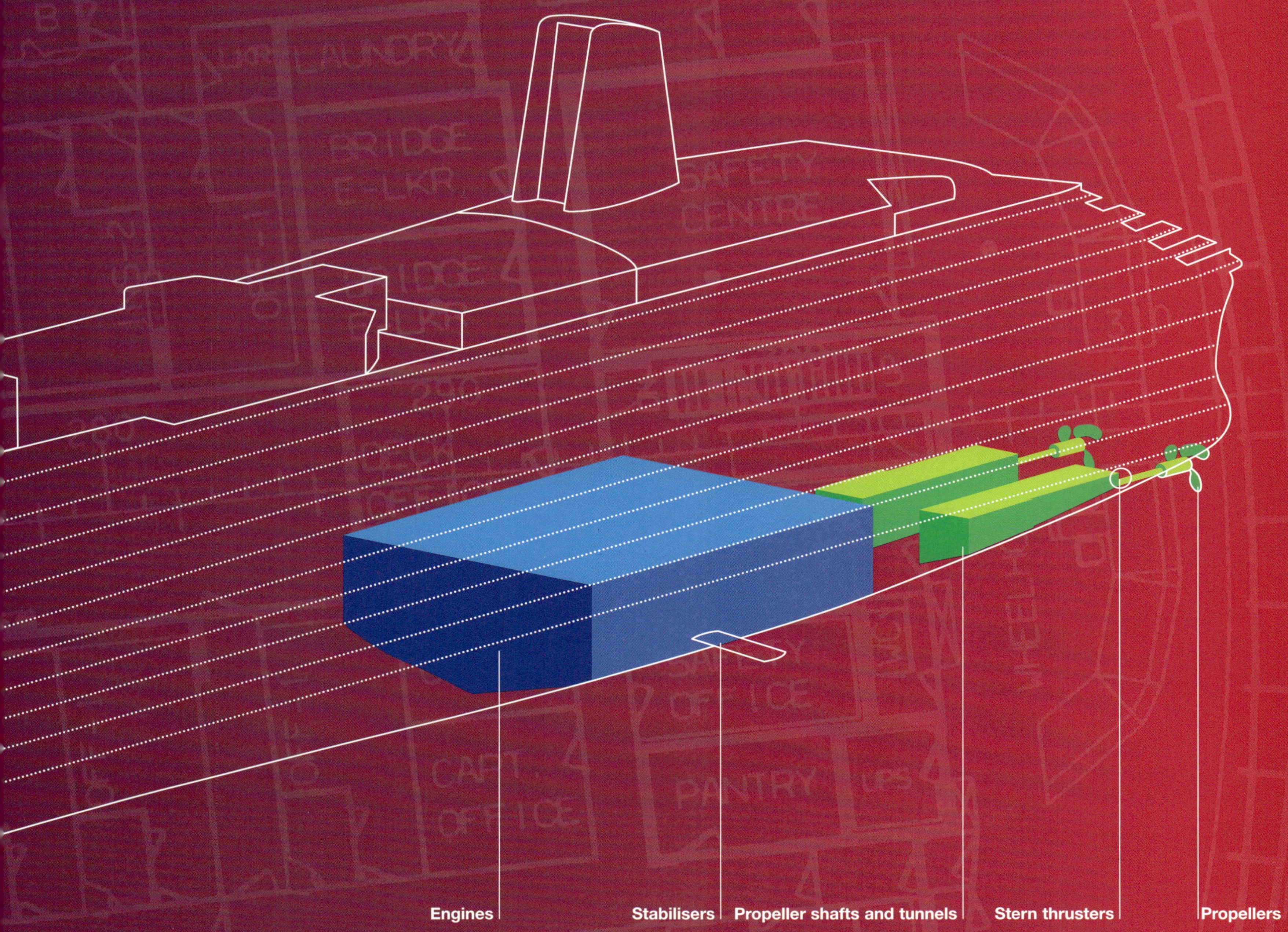
Engines
Stabilisers
Propeller shafts and tunnels
Stern thrusters
Propellers

Sixty feet above the water-line, P&O's crest, the sun rising out of the sea in the East, shines down newly painted. *Aurora* is preparing to leave the yard where she was built. Soon she will be at sea. Behind the gleaming white paint is an immensely strong structure. Welders, whose work is checked first by the yard, then by experts from Lloyd's Register (which guarantees *Aurora*'s quality to her insurers) and finally by P&O, work on the inverted stem section of the liner's bow. The steel is thicker than a warship's and the welds are stronger than the steel they join.

The bows are craned into place and welded fast. *Aurora*'s stem is sharp above the waterline to slice through rough seas, but the waves a ship's hull create always waste energy. So the hydrodynamicists design a huge underwater bulb, shaped rather like a dolphin's nose, to produce a secondary wave which will tend to cancel the ordinary bow wave. The crest of one falls into the trough of the other. *Aurora* will slip more easily through the water. And the bulbous bow, cavernous inside, makes useful space for ballast tanks.

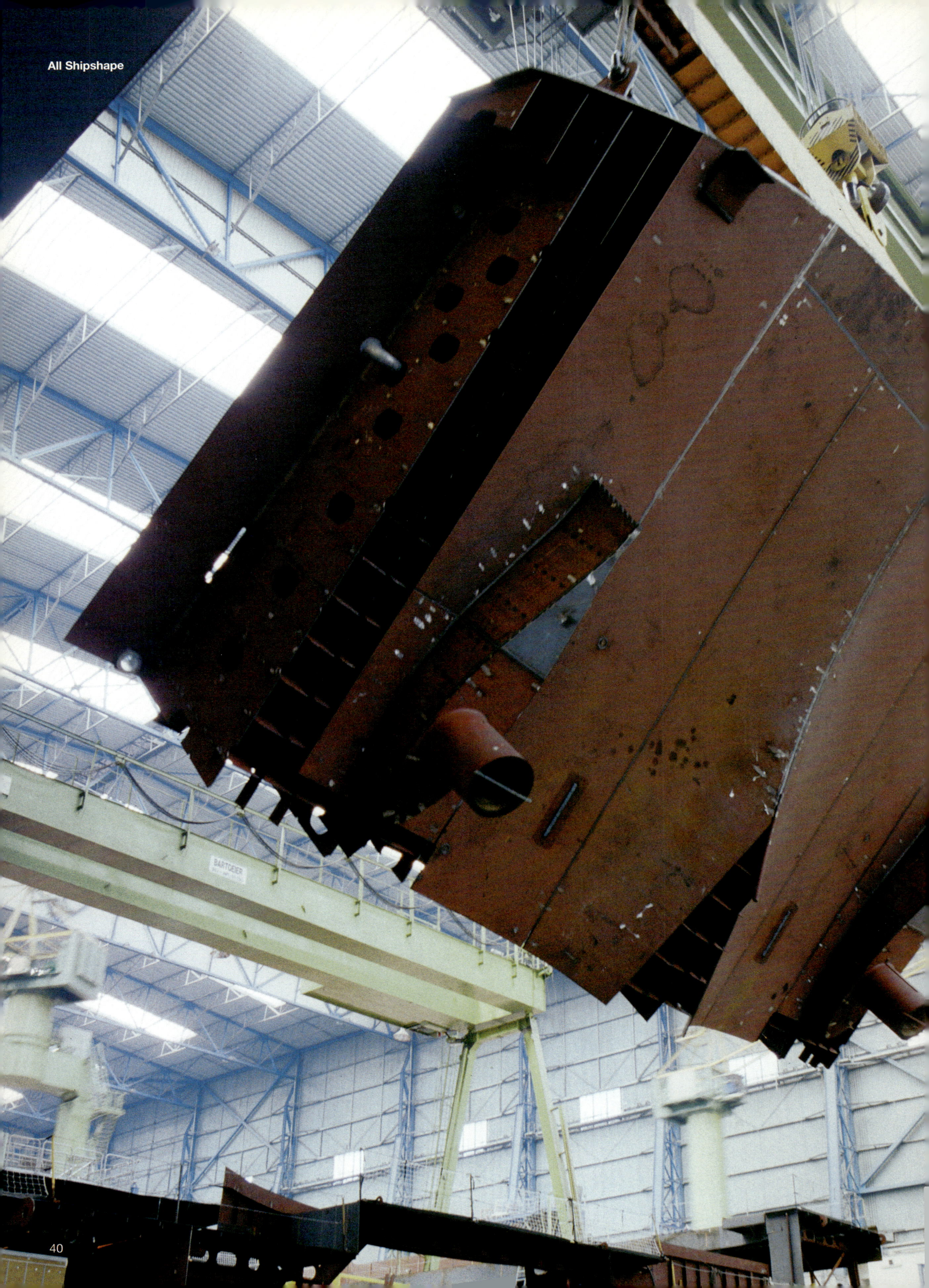

A herring's eye view from beneath the stern. The aftermost part of the ship's bottom is lowered into place in the dry building dock. *Aurora* is steered by two great rudders, built by Becker of Hamburg. They will be fitted into bearing tubes in the fish-shaped fairings on Block 41 and hang just behind the ship's main propellers. The sparkling four-bladed screw seen here is one of four side thrusters which nudge the vessel into and out of harbour.

A welder works on the great starboard rudder. The two pierced steel drums beyond him are dummy ('zero-thrust') propellers which are fitted while *Aurora* is being built to test the engines. They can be run in water in the flooded dock without moving the ship.

The first of the two five-bladed main propellers has arrived from Sweden. Made of nickel aluminium bronze alloy, it weighs over 20 tonnes. Each blade has an area of about 4 square metres (43 sq. ft.) and its complex curves are designed to translate the massive power of *Aurora*'s electric motors into smooth forward motion. It is a pity that no passenger will ever see the propellers' lovely shapes, but everyone will appreciate their silent, vibrationless efficiency.

The funnel is lifted into position, its upper edge 53 metres (174 ft.) above the waterline. Although the casing is made of aluminium, the whole unit weighs 64 tonnes and it encloses a mass of different pipes and ducts. *Aurora*'s four main diesel engines are very clean-burning, but the hot gases from each 1,500 litre power-plant must be discharged by the four exhaust pipes, each 1.2 metres (4 ft.) in diameter, high above and behind the decks. Heat which would otherwise be wasted is recovered in the funnel by exhaust gas boilers which generate useful steam, heating bath water and warming rooms on chilly days. Even the extractors above the galley's stoves exhaust through the funnel. This is no ordinary chimney pot.

Aurora Bridge Visit
Information Sheet

Aurora was built at the Meyer Werft shipyard in Papenburg, Germany. She sailed on her maiden voyage on the 1st May 2000, a few days after her naming by Her Royal Highness The Princess Royal.

The Vessel's name comes from the ancient Greek mythology, Aurora (also known as Eos) was the Goddess of the Dawn. Every morning she rose from the ocean into the sky signifying sunrise as she rode across the sky in a purple horse drawn chariot.

The Aurora is equipped with an STN Atlas Marine Integrated Bridge System (IBS). An IBS is a combination of systems which are inter-connected to allow the monitoring of sensor information and control of a number of operations, such as passage execution, communications, machinery control, safety and security. The IBS ensures that information is presented in the most efficient way to the Captain and his watch keeping officers. The following pieces of equipment are among those from which information is drawn.
Global Positioning System (GPS) – Speed and Position Information
Echo sounder – Depth
Gyrocompass – Course
E.C.D.I.S. – Electronic Chart Display and Information System

STATISTICS AND TECHNICAL DATA

Name: Aurora	Call Sign: ZCDW9
Country of Registry: Bermuda	Port of Choice: Hamilton
Gross Tonnage: 76,152t	Length Overall: 272.1m
Extreme Breadth: 40.35m	Draught: 8.4m
Air Draught: 53.48m	Service Speed: 24kts
Stopping Distance at 24kts: 0.85nm	Stopping Distance at 15kts: 0.4nm
Engines: 4 Medium Speed Diesels	Propellers: 2 Fixed Pitch
Stabilisers: 2	Bow Thrusters: 3 x 1,500Kw
Stern Thruster: 1 x 1,500Kw	Rudders: 2 spade independent
Crew 850	Passengers 1950

Power
Each of Aurora's 4 MAN B&W diesel generators, generate 13650Kw of power – approximately 18200bhp. When all four engines are at maximum load, this is about 72800bhp - equivalent to1300 small family cars, or 92 Ferrari Formula One racing cars. These generators supply electricity to the propulsion motors and all shipboard services. Aurora's four transverse thrusters generate 2000bhp each, the same as having 140 small family hatchbacks moving her sideways on and off the berth. These thrusters mean that tug boats are not normally required to dock and undock the ship.
In terms of electricity generated, the total power output from all 4 generators on maximum load would light up nearly 1 million household 60-watt light bulbs. This is enough electricity to power a town the size of Oxford.

Fuel
Aurora's V-type 14 cylinder engines run on Heavy Fuel Oil rather than petrol or diesel. Each will consume about 40 litres of fuel per minute or 60 tonnes per day. With all 4 engines running at maximum load this is enough for Aurora to steam 580 nautical miles at maximum speed.
This works out at approximately 1/80th of a statute mile to the gallon, or 67 feet to the gallon.

Water
The Technical Department on board Aurora endeavour to produce all of Aurora's fresh water on board. Our 2 Fresh Water Generators (or Evaporators) can each make 26.6 tonnes of fresh water every hour. Between the two, this is about 1280 tonnes per day, enough to fill all of Aurora's swimming pools and Jacuzzi Whirlpools over 4 times each day.

Assisted by four tugs, the great white ship creeps at a walking pace down the narrow River Ems towards the sea. The river has been specially dredged in places for her passage. *Aurora* has a shallow draft to enable her to visit as many ports as possible in her cruising career and she is burdened by little fuel or ballast, but the river is only just deep enough at high water and the tide will ebb during her journey. She has to moor halfway down river and wait for it to rise again.

The yard's captain, Friedhelm Husemeyer, has done this transit many times before, but he and the pilots assisting him have rehearsed on a computer-driven simulator for hours so that they are perfectly prepared for the most difficult parts of the passage.

P&O captains are used to sailing through the Suez Canal and they can turn their ships on a sixpence in a crowded harbour, but none of them would envy Herr Husemeyer as he squeezed Ship 640 (soon to be named *Aurora*) through the lifting bridge at the village of Weener. An unexpected puff of wind could have spelled disaster; but all goes well and two hours before dawn she is safely moored at Eemshaven.

All Shipshape

Chief Technical Officer Paul Clasby is qualified to drive a steam locomotive – railways are his hobby – but he is glad that *Aurora* derives her power from reliable diesels, even if they are noisy and steam was silent. Earlier generations of P&O engineers struggled to keep their engine rooms clean while coal dust and ashes crept into the bearings and under a man's skin. In the boiler rooms, their stokers heaved tons of coal in such hellish temperatures that they earned special rations.

Second Engineer Officer David Russell leans out of the crankcase of one of the two main diesels to reach a micrometer. He is measuring any elongation of the bottom end bearing bolts. Routine maintenance is done in port with one engine closed down and the other running to maintain power for the 'hotel side'.

On Number One deck, deep below the water level, one of the two massive shafts transmit the power of *Aurora*'s electric motors to the propellers.

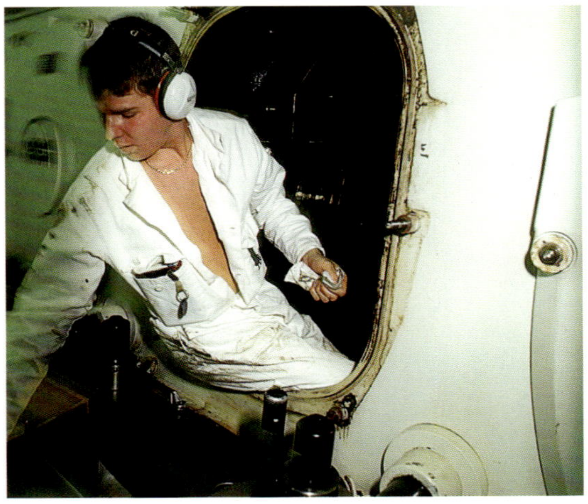

Not yet officially called *Aurora*, the ship sails purposefully into the North Sea for her sea trials. She flies no flags and the P&O officers aboard as observers make a point of wearing civilian clothes in deference to her German crew; for until she is formally handed over, Ship 640 still belongs to Meyer Werft and the yard's men are still in command.

From the P&O helicopter hovering ahead of the ship, the vertical windows of the two penthouses can clearly be seen, just below the bridge, offering a lucky few the finest private vantage points aboard.

Below decks, hundreds of workmen put the finishing touches to her furnishings, lay carpets and apply the last coats of paint. In the engine rooms, every system is checked and re-checked. There are smiles on the bridge. The ship works perfectly. Soon she will belong to P&O.

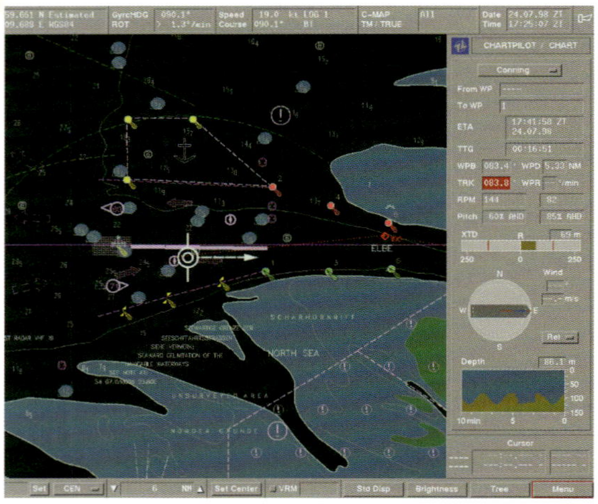

The bridge takes shape in the Papenburg yard. A chain fence protects shipyard workers until the gaping windows are glazed. The first cables are laid. Thousands of metres of wire will connect the bridge with every part of the ship; up to the radars and radios on the deck above, down to the engine room; through to every department, for the bridge is *Aurora*'s brain, the centre of her nervous system. On the deckhead, ducts reach out to where the air-conditioning vents will breathe cool air over the officers and extract hot air from the powerful navigational and communications equipment of the modern ship. *Aurora* is cool, automated and electronic.

Despite radar so detailed that its colour display looks like a page in your road atlas, the Captain turns to the Admiralty chart for detailed information about the harbour *Aurora* is soon to enter and the Navigator will still plot the ship's progress on the traditional chart, just in case.

Creatur

e Comforts

Penthouse suites
The acme of luxury aboard *Aurora*. The two-storey Penthouse Suites have incomparable views ahead of the ship and private balconies on both decks. There is dining space for six (your butler will serve at table), a bar area and guests' cloakroom. One Penthouse Suite has a baby grand piano which will play itself when you tire of playing it; the other has a large library of music CDs and spoken-word tapes. (Penthouse Suites offer about 865 sq. ft. of room space).

Staterooms with balconies
Staterooms are larger than cabins, slightly smaller than suites. The bathrooms have bath, shower and WC. There is a separate sitting area and king-size or twin beds, as you prefer. While on the private balcony is room for a lounger, chair and table. (Staterooms offer about 210 sq. ft. of room space).

Cabins with balconies
40% of *Aurora*'s cabins have private balconies and the Twin Cabin with Balcony is a new category for P&O Cruises. It allows passengers to experience the pleasures of a private balcony (39 sq. ft. extra space) for less than the price of a Stateroom. A queen-size bed (or singles if you prefer) and a bath or shower, calm blues and dusky pinks, cherry-wood veneers, original art and the detailed attention to convenience typical of P&O ships would make this a very attractive cabin choice. The balcony makes it exceptional. (Twin Cabins with Balcony offer about 175 sq. ft. of room space).

Cabins without balconies
Even the most economical cabins aboard *Aurora* offer great comfort and convenience. Every one has its own bathroom and they are all air-conditioned. There is a mini fridge, tea/coffee making facilities (though of course you get a steward too) a TV, phone and a small safe. The cabins are brilliantly designed to give you lots of space and are decorated to seem even larger than they are. Some have Pullman-style berths for a third or fourth occupant (at very special rates); others are available for single occupancy. (Cabins without balconies offer about 150 sq. ft. of room space).

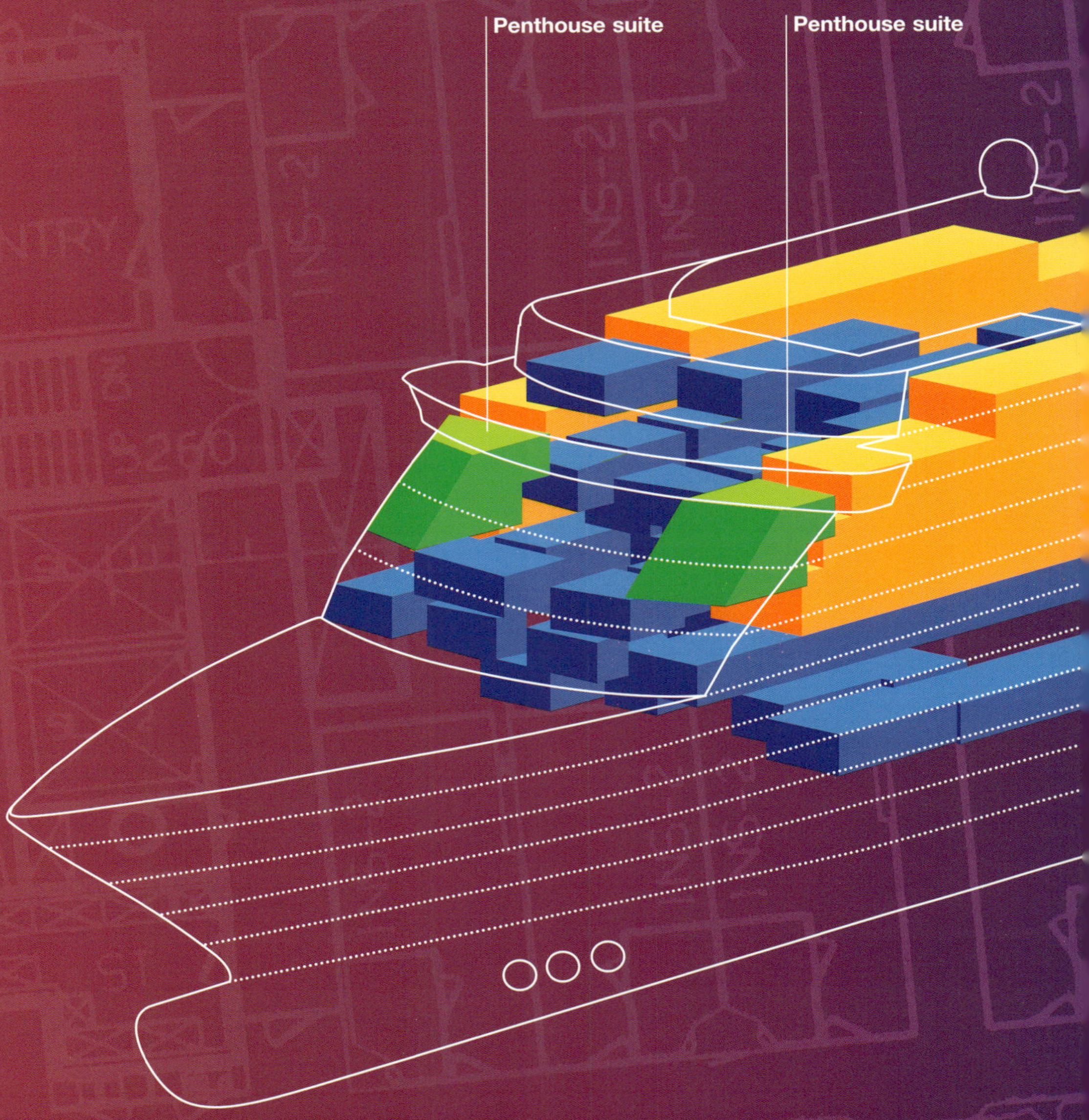

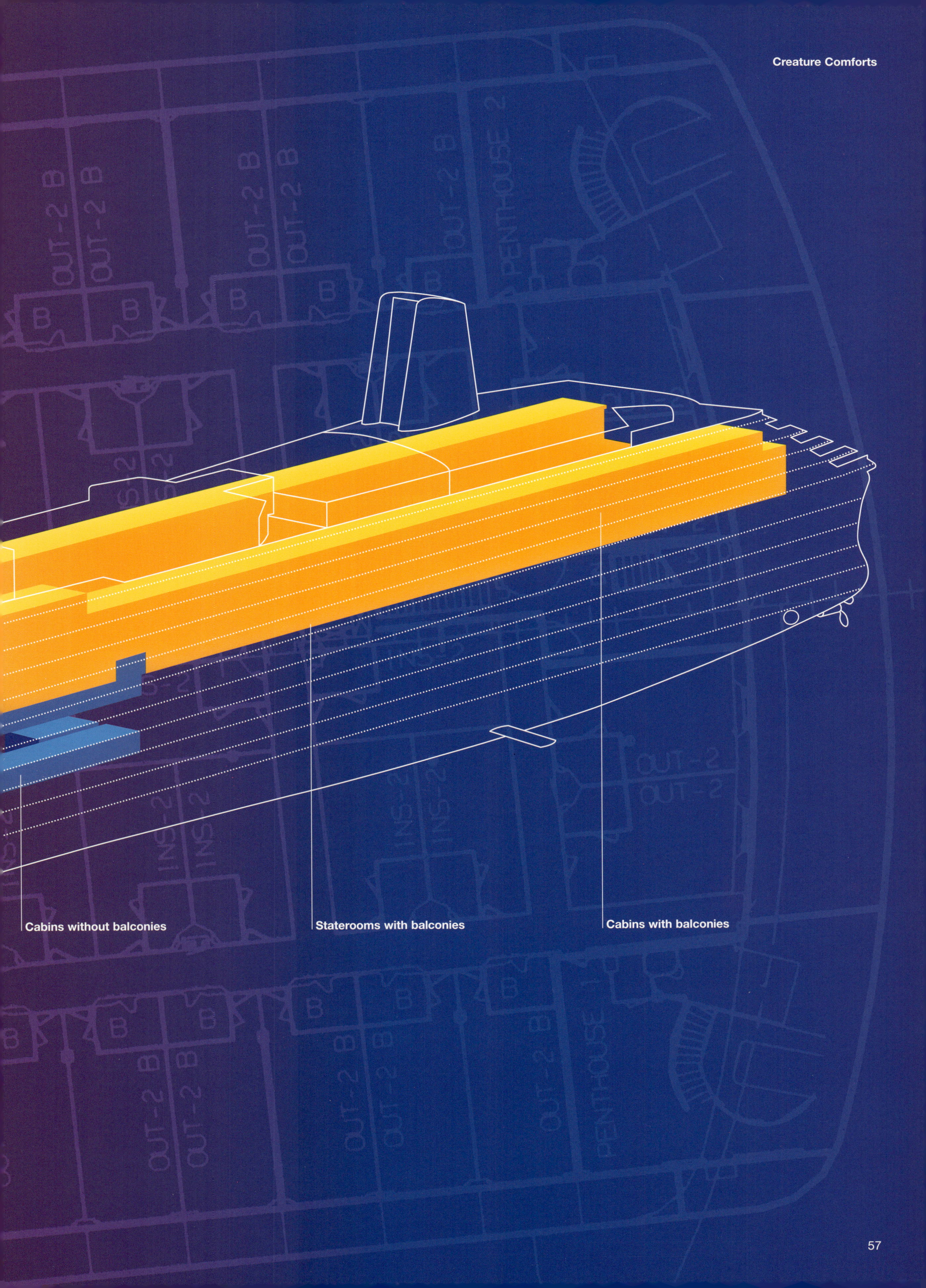
Cabins without balconies
Staterooms with balconies
Cabins with balconies

LUMINAIRE
DE SECURITE

In the warm Summer of 1999, the last prefabricated block is towed up the River Ems from the Bremerhaven works where it was built. The journey is slow but Block 51 is precisely on time. As soon as it reaches Papenburg, the 200 tonne box of unpainted steel is hoisted into place. It fits perfectly because the machine which cut the steel plates 60km away in Bremerhaven was controlled by the IBM computer in the Meyer Werft design office. Welders fix it to the other blocks and the fitters begin their work. Soon Block 51, still just a part of Hull 640, will become a section of *Aurora*'s balcony cabins and suites.

When P&O first sailed to Bombay in the 1840s, Indians were hired because it was thought that they were better able to stand the heat in the engine rooms. Very soon it became clear that many were skilled seamen. Nowadays Bombay has become Mumbai and there, in the P&O Training School, new recruits are given the first stages of their training as stewards and junior galley staff. For while *Aurora*'s Engine Ratings are now nearly all from the Philippines, and the Deck Ratings are Pakistani, the Hotel Department is still almost entirely staffed by calm, skilled, impeccably mannered Indians.

Lili Mora from Budapest turns down the beds in one of the 14 cabins for which she is responsible. About a fifth of *Aurora*'s 67 cabin stewards are from Eastern Europe and most have worked in tourist hotels ashore before learning the special skills needed by a P&O steward. From early morning tea and breakfast trays to the evening turndown, cabin stewards work long hours. Their reward lies in really getting to know 'their' passengers and helping them enjoy the cruise.

The bathrooms in *Aurora*'s cabins are miracles of compact convenience. Like a conjuring trick, every mirror reveals more space, another useful compartment. They all have a loo and a shower; many have a bath; some are adapted for disabled people; all are safe, floored with non-slip materials and well provided with handles and rails. It is easy for the steward to make them sparkle for you. She'll bring you wonderfully fluffy towels whenever you need them too.

Every cabin aboard *Aurora* offers a degree of comfort and convenience that most people only dream about. The staterooms, like this one (right) offer extra space. There is 100 sq. ft. more room than in a twin cabin (which most people think wonderfully spacious). There is a separate sitting area with a sofa, a table and chair. And being *Aurora*, the ship with far more balconies than most other ships, you have only to step through the floor-to-ceiling patio doors to be on your own private balcony. If the bed was not so comfortable looking one would never think of leaving the lounger on the balcony until the sun set. And even then, what a place to watch the lights on the shore with a glass in your hand while your partner gets ready for the evening!

The Penthouse Suites are uniquely large and luxurious. The Piano Suite (above) is the most opulent and spacious accommodation on board. Only the Library Suite on the other side of the ship can equal it. On two decks, with its own sweeping staircase and incomparable views ahead through tall windows, two private balconies and 865 sq. ft. of luxury and convenience, the Penthouse Suites take you into millionaire country, but you really don't have to win the Lottery to try them. Spoil yourself. Just once.

Sun on B

right Water

Skydome
There are days, even on a P&O cruise, when the sun won't shine and still you feel like a swim. Then a canopy of clear glass almost as wide as the ship is slid over the Crystal Pool and you can enjoy yourself in the warmth of an indoor pool. The moment the sun comes out, the Skydome slides open again.

Crystal Pool
Amidships on Lido deck (12) is the largest pool on *Aurora*. The Crystal Pool is over 10 metres (32 ft.) long and nearly 6 metres (19 ft.) wide. It has two whirlpool spas beside it and a fine bar. Around the pool on two levels there is plenty of space for those who want nothing more energetic than to watch other people swimming, while basking in the sun.

Riviera Pool
High on Lido deck, but carefully sheltered from the wind, the Riviera Pool will tempt sun worshippers from the terraces which surround it. Over 9 metres (29 ft.) long and nearly 6 metres (19 ft.) wide, there is room for almost everyone in the sparkling clean, slightly heated water. And to add to their pleasure, the water spills over a gentle waterfall, beside which there is a whirlpool spa and the Riviera Bar.

Oasis
Between the two pools on Lido deck is the Oasis Health and Beauty Spa where there are five treatment rooms and a nine-chair hairdressing salon. The decorative theme of Oasis is botanical. The aim is refreshment, relaxation and rejuvenation. The methods include sauna and steam room, facials, manicures, pedicures, massages, aromatherapy, and thalasso-therapy.

Weighs & Measures
You do not have to be a body builder to benefit from the gym and exercise studio on Arcadia deck (11). It has a superb range of cardiovascular and weight training equipment. A trained and sympathetic instructor will help you find the right fitness programme for your age and capabilities, and will check that you are exercising safely and effectively.

Toybox/Jumping Jacks/Quarterdeck/ Decibel's/Intergalactica
Aurora is one of the world's best-equipped ships for young families. Clustered around the Terrace Pool area are special brightly decorated rooms for under-five's, six-to-nines, a den with a disco for young teens and Decibels, where older teenagers can be as noisy as they like. A night nursery and an interactive games centre provide for the sleepy and the techno-young.

Terrace pool
Aurora's third pool overlooks the stern on Devanha deck (8). It is surrounded by the children's rooms and is normally reserved for families. There is a safe paddling pool for the smallest passengers and whirlpool spas for the adults.

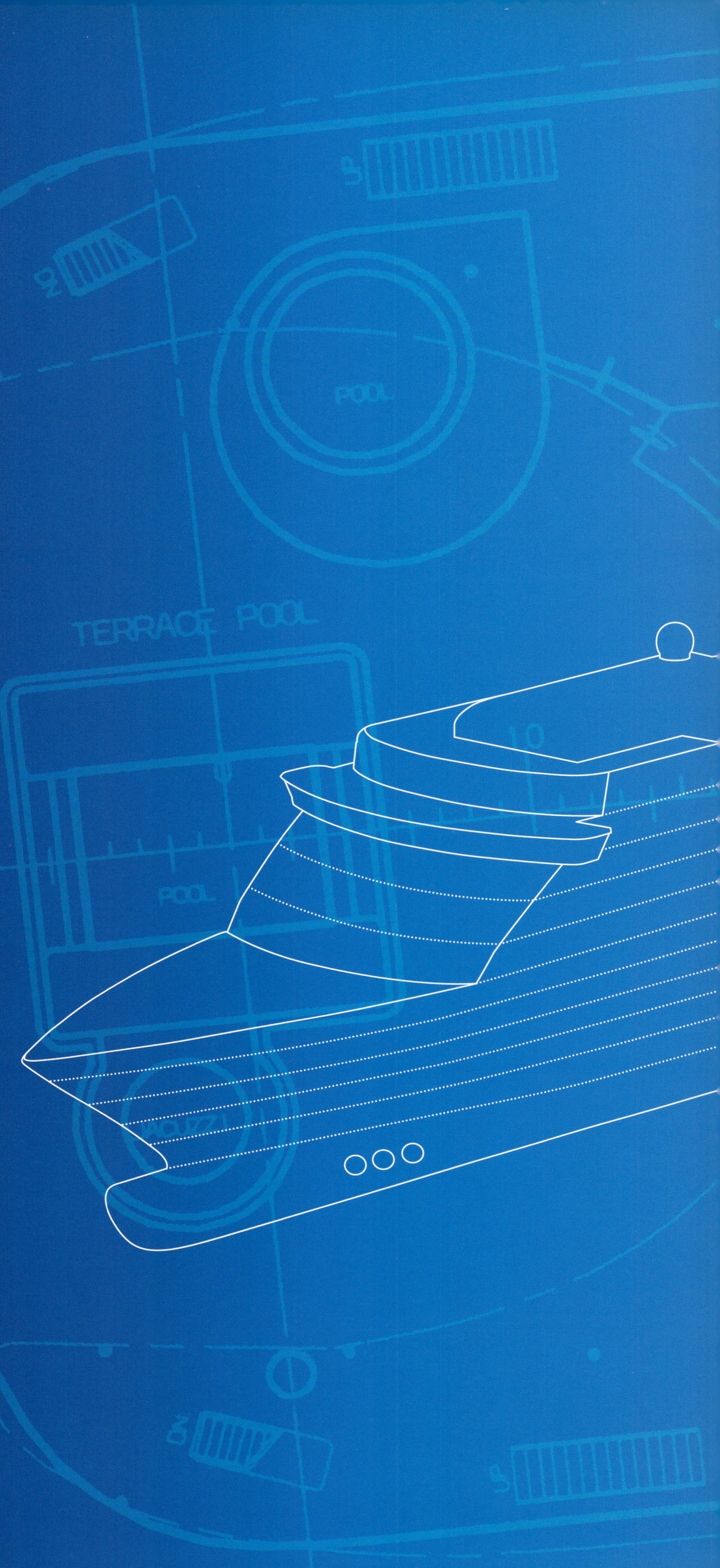

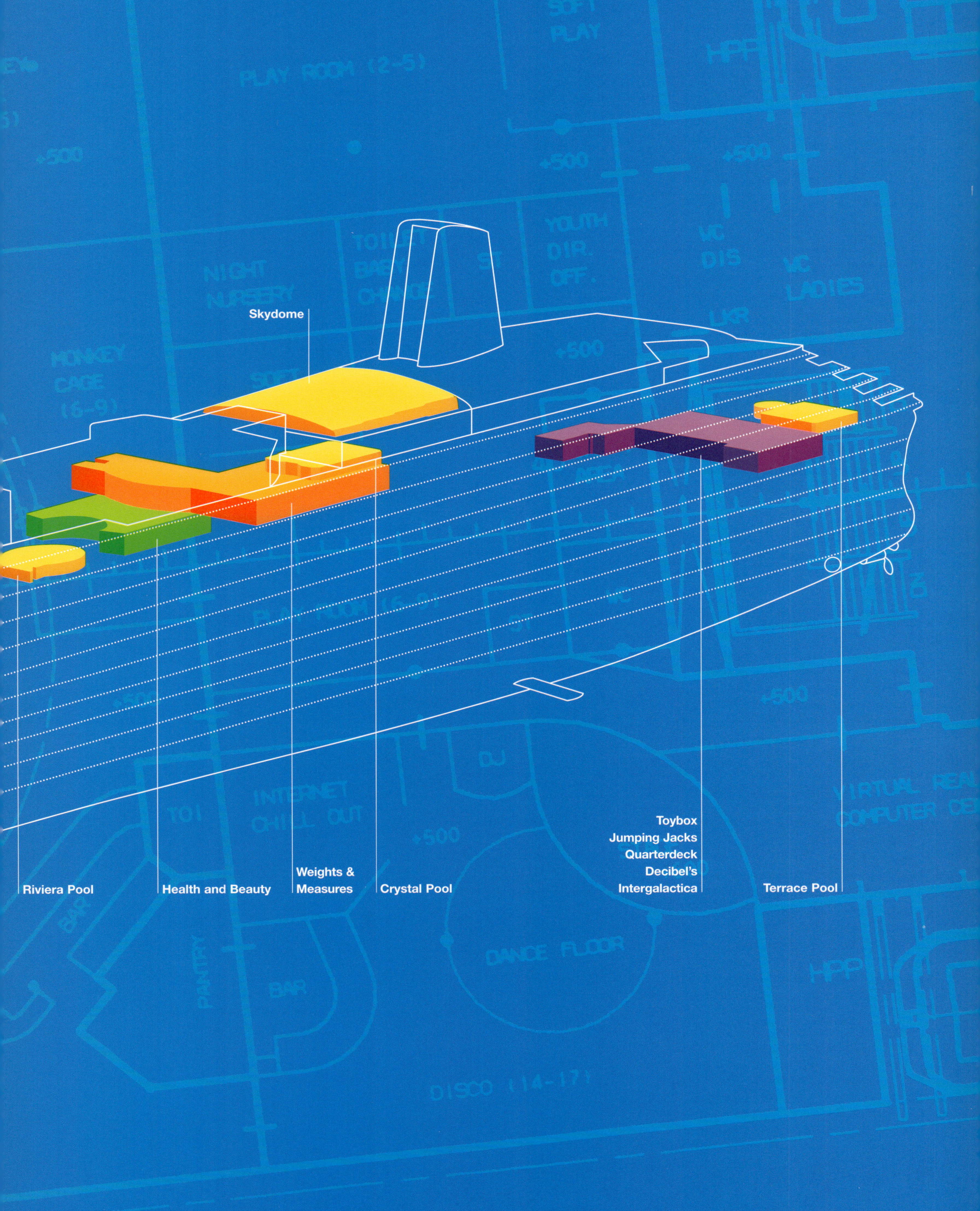
Skydome
Riviera Pool
Health and Beauty
Weights &
Measures
Crystal Pool
Toybox
Jumping Jacks
Quarterdeck
Decibel's
Intergalactica
Terrace Pool

A shipyard worker inspects the steelwork which will frame the Riviera Pool on the Lido deck. *Aurora*'s three swimming pools, children's paddling pool and four jacuzzis use a lot of water, but every day the ship's state-of-the-art desalination and cleaning plant freshens 1,200 tonnes of sea water into crystal-clear water that's good enough to drink. The water in the pools is treated to be kind to your skin and hair too.

When you are ten, the Centre of the Universe is the Terrace Pool. If you can get onto the cross-bar and stay there for more than a minute, you know what Heaven is like. And what if one of the boys does push you off? You can ignore him this evening when the Centre of the Universe moves to the Quarterdeck.

The pool is safe because it is supervised and because it has been designed with safety in mind. Little children can't open the gates which surround it; fences are made so they can't be climbed; and there is non-slip material on the deck. So the fun isn't spoiled by tears and Heaven is – just Heaven.

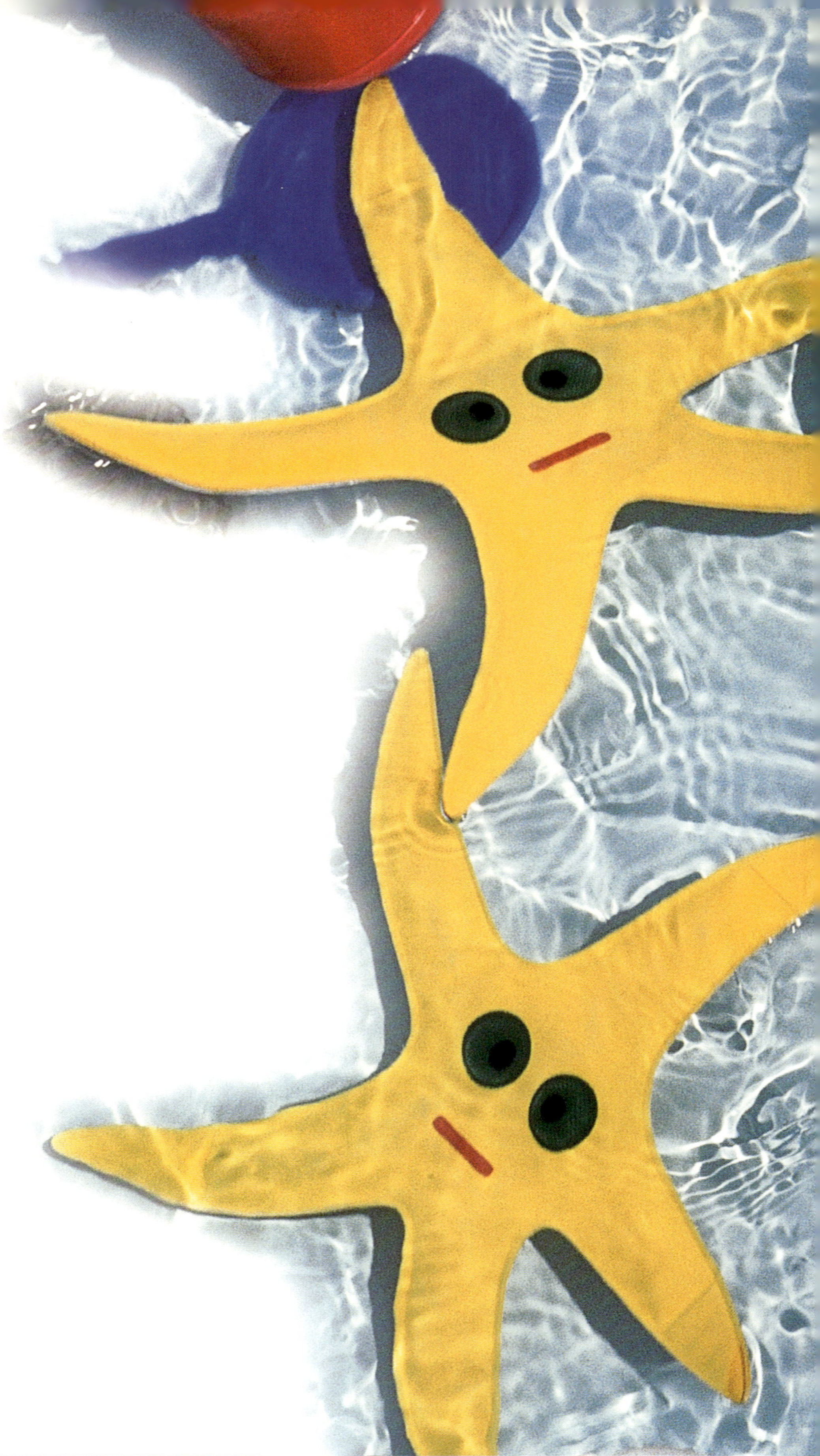

Safe, busy and very happy; they're learning too. Mum's dream? Well she can nod off if she wants to because the Youth Crew have the day planned and the children want to be part of it. They are in charge. From nine in the morning until 10.30pm small children play. Sport and entertainment is non-stop in the *Toybox* and *Jumping Jacks* playrooms. There is a children's paddling pool too. And when it's bedtime, a supervised Night Nursery so parents can dance until two in the morning. This is the reality of a family holiday on *Aurora*. Or is it a dream?

Skillfully chipping away at a huge block of ice, the most artistic chef in *Aurora*'s galley gradually discovers a dolphin in his melting medium. Passengers on deck around him have fun guessing what the outcome will be. Could it be from one of Rudyard Kipling's *Just So Stories*; 'How the Elephant got his Trunk?' Who knows? By teatime it will have melted away.

Sculptor Allan Sly's *Pearl Diver*, beside the Crystal Pool, was five months in the making and will last forever. Modelled in clay it was then cast in bronze and carefully 'patinated' to give it a greeny-black sheen. The piece weighs 350 kg, but is so carefully balanced that the diver looks almost weightless. Many a passenger around the pool wishes that they were too.

An informal themed lunch is often served on the Lido Deck around the Pennant Bar. This is Neptune's Buffet. Tridents come neatly wrapped and someone in the galley – perhaps *Aurora*'s ice carver? – knows how to make terrestrial vegetables look like the prettiest sea-anemones. A senior chef-de-partie brings another box of langoustines or Dublin Bay prawns to the serving table. There are succulent oysters and the largest, tenderest mussels too, fresh salads and rolls crisp enough to tempt a mermaid to join the ladies who lunch.

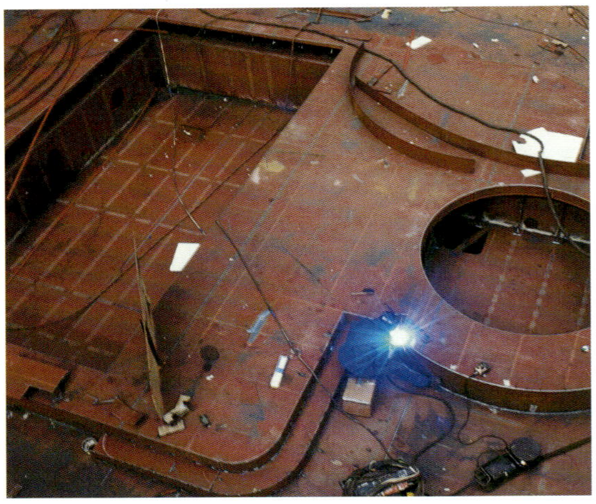

In 1968 Roy Jacuzzi gave his name to the world by inventing the whirlpool bath. There are two whirlpool spas beside the Crystal Pool and others by the Terrace and Riviera Pools. The Jacuzzi family came to California from Italy, so perhaps we ought to say their name like pizza? Or let's worry about that later over a slice of that Italian pie in the Sidewalk Café.

When the sun shines and the air is warm there are three pools to choose from aboard *Aurora*. On cooler days most people will make for the largest. The Crystal Pool can be covered at the touch of a button by a glazed Skydome which slides over the pool and the poolside area. Like an enormous conservatory it lets in the sun, keeps out the chilly breezes.

You might not think that many of the passengers on this cruise had retired, though Grandpa is 82. He says that the sea air is rejuvenating. His daughter wonders what might have given him this new lease of life. Whatever the cause, he has never felt so well. His granddaughter (aged 14) is really pleased that all three generations of the family are on holiday together. As she says, it's brilliant. There are lots of people her age on board too. Cruising is becoming a younger holiday and *Aurora* is the ship which appeals most to the younger style-conscious part of the market.

Solid planks of Thai teak (*tectona grandis*), obtained from renewable sources, are laid over the steel deck structure. The caulker is taking a break. It is hard laying *Aurora*'s 3,730 square metres (40,149 sq. ft.) of wooden deck, even when wearing knee protectors. The hammer is used to firm the sealing material (caulk) between the boards.

Shuffleboard (or shovelboard) was popular in England in the 14th century, especially with the aristocracy. Shove-ha'penny, still played in traditional pubs, is the indoor version. But the modern game was defined in St Petersburg, Florida in 1924.

She's playing tennis on deck, but it isn't deck tennis. The old ship's game with a rope quoit began when P&O passengers on their way to India adapted the great craze of 1874 for lawn tennis to small decks. Today there's room for both.

An empty sun-lounger casts an abstract pattern on the non-slip deck surface around the Crystal Pool. Safety comes first, so where the deck is likely to be wet, the traditional teak decking gives way to modern polymers. The same coating is used on the cabin and stateroom balconies.

A footprint on the deck highlights one of the charms of traditional teak; it darkens when damp to a brownish-grey, then bleaches as it dries. If you are up very early when the decks are being swabbed you may catch a hint of the timber's aromatic fragrance too. Ships' decks are laid in teak because of the timber's extremely good dimensional stability; wet or dry, hot or cold, it hardly shrinks or expands.

Hard at work in the Weights and Measures gym on Arcadia deck (11), passengers of all ages puff and pant on the cardiovascular machines. Rowing, Nordic skiing and bicycling rapidly up hill is particularly good for you if you have had just a little too much to eat the night before and it is satisfying to see on the electronic displays how many calories are disappearing! The keep-fitters are confident about what they are doing because it is carefully supervised by trained fitness instructors. After the gym or aerobic session, the ladies relax in the hairdresser's. The men are probably weightlifting in the bar.

Move

able Feasts

Sidewalk Café
Between the Riviera and Crystal pools; conveniently close to the Oasis health and beauty centre; the Sidewalk Café serves snacks such as burgers, pizza, salads and open sandwiches. You will find light meals such as grills there too from late morning until early evening.

Raffles
Close to the library, Cyb@study and Vanderbilt's games room is a small bar for addicts of chocolate and coffee. Throughout the day and late into the evening, Raffles serves hand-made chocolates, liqueurs and speciality coffees.

The Orangery
The Orangery self-service restaurant is large, informal and opens early. There is easy access to the surrounding decks and there are many sheltered tables with a fine view - this restaurant is 80 feet above the water-line. The Orangery serves a full English breakfast, buffet lunches and afternoon teas with cakes like Mother used to make. And in the evening, softer lighting and the opening of a dance floor transform The Orangery into the perfect setting for a themed dinner.

Café Bordeaux
On the deck above Champions sports bar and connected to it by a broad spiral staircase, Café Bordeaux is open 24 hours a day. The food is French (croissants or brioches at breakfast, croque-monsieur or salade niçoise at lunch, onion soup or tarte Tatin in the small hours); the atmosphere that of a traditional bistro.

Medina Restaurant
One of the two great formal dining-rooms aboard, the Medina Restaurant seats 528 at tables for between two and 10 guests. Places are reserved for dinner, but for breakfast, luncheon and afternoon tea, passengers sit where they like. Large windows on either side make the room bright during the day and allow glimpses of the moonlit sea at night. A feature staircase sweeps down into the restaurant (but there is level entry for everyone who wants it). The room is decorated in a Moorish style reflecting P&O's traditional connections with North Africa and the Middle East.

Alexandria Restaurant
Aurora's other formal dining room, the Alexandria Restaurant, seats 520, a few at tables for couples, most in larger friendly groups of up to ten. Large windows round the stern frame superb views and allow a sparkling sun or moonlight to be reflected into the room from the ship's wake. Here the theme of the decoration is Egyptian, but the food is classic.

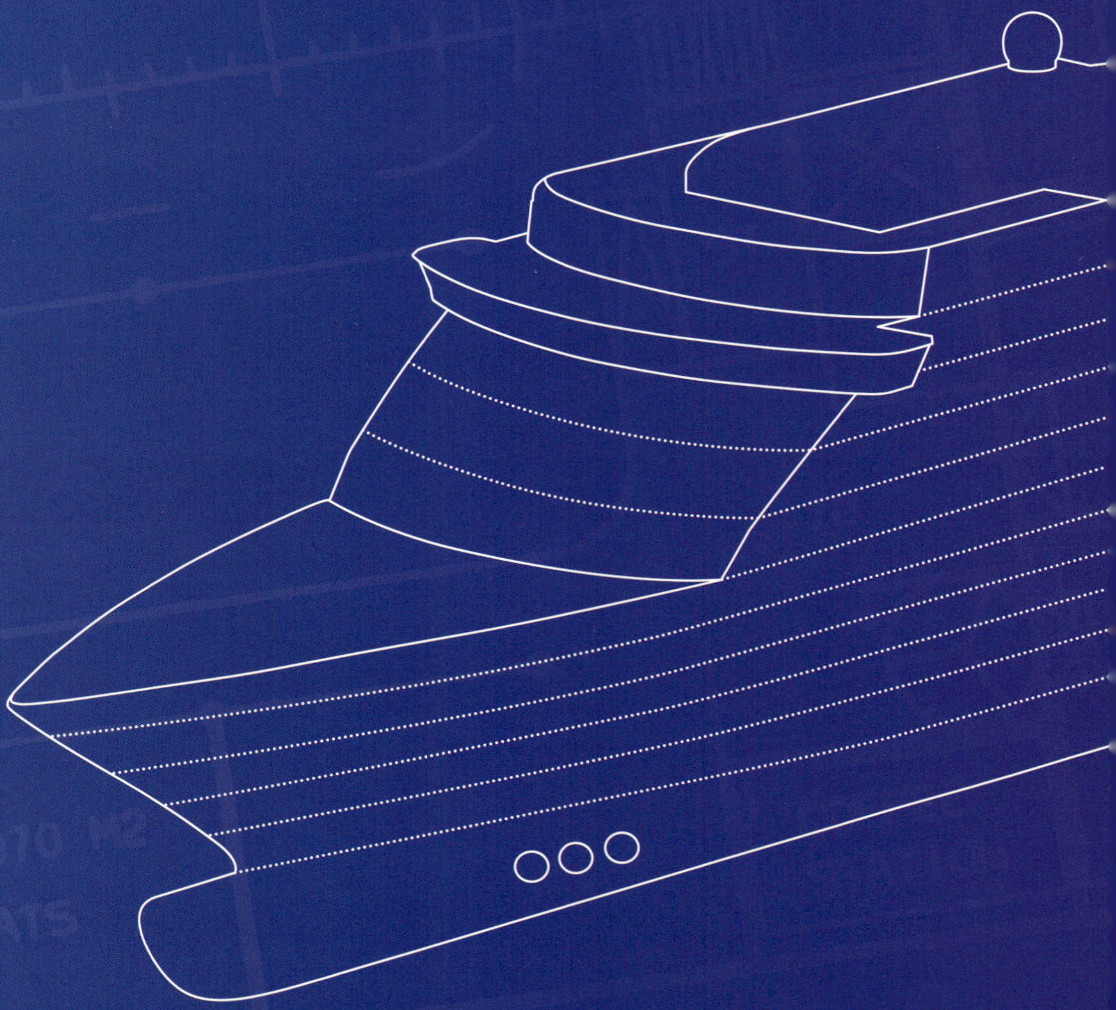

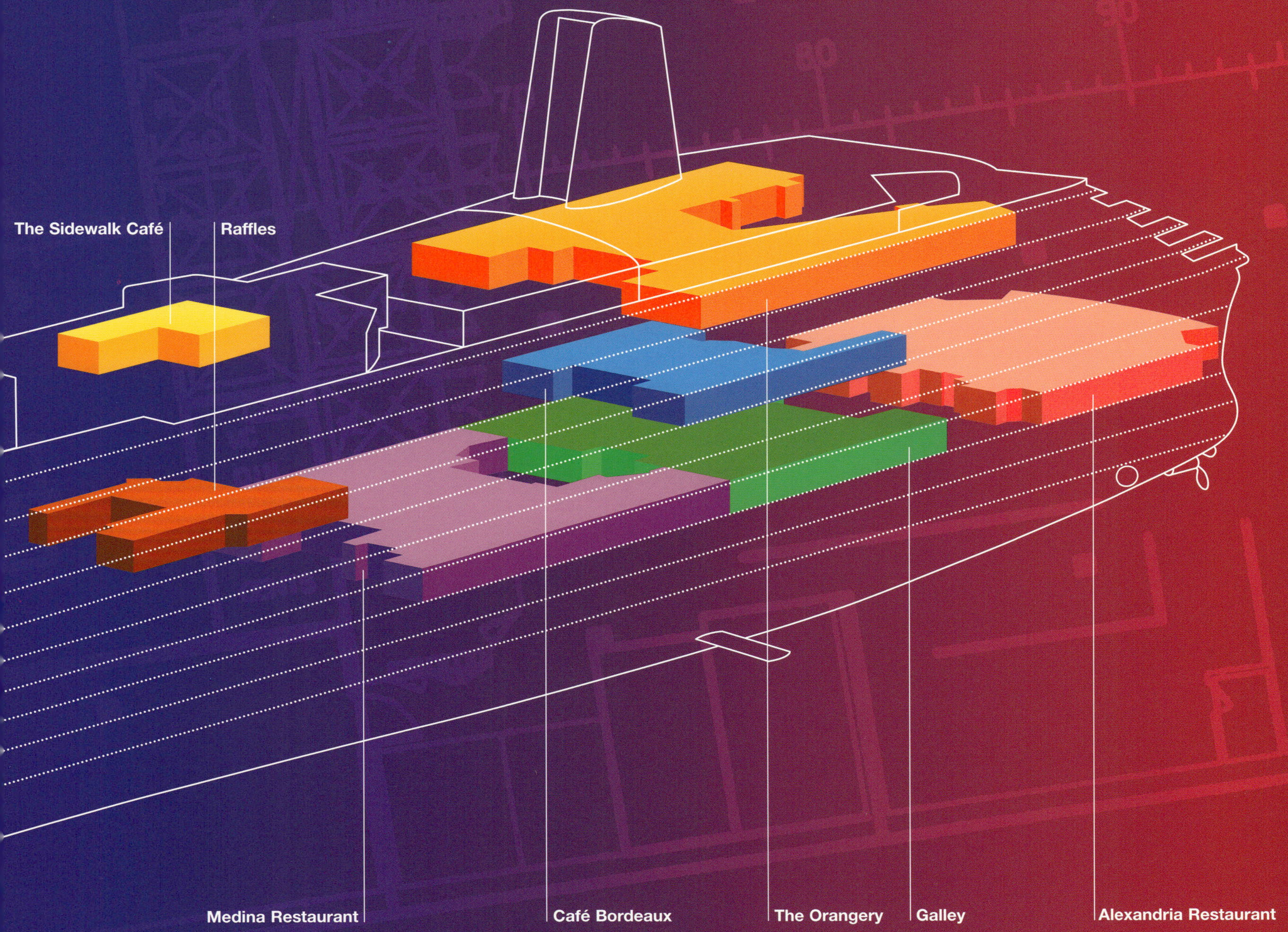
The Sidewalk Café
Raffles
Medina Restaurant
Café Bordeaux
The Orangery
Galley
Alexandria Restaurant

The galley brigade is led by Executive Chef Haydn Davis, seen here talking to one of the sous chefs. The team ('brigade') have French titles, traditional in the catering industry; so there are sous chefs, chefs-de-partie and commis waiters in the Galley. The Head Butcher, Head Baker and Executive Pastry Chef are exceptions to the general rule. Haydn supervises 132 people, all specialising in some part of the process of feeding the 2,815 people who may be aboard – and of clearing up afterwards, for 28 of the people in the galley are rated Utility Hand (Platehouse) and that means that they wash up.

Premier Sous Chef Ronan Hart knows that the only way to tell if a dish tastes as good as it looks is to try it. Every detail of how the food is presented has been discussed with Executive Chef Haydn Davis and the commis, chefs-de-partie and assistants who plate up the food when the rush of orders come in know precisely what is wanted. *Aurora*'s galley serves about 12,000 main meals a day.

The decoration of the Medina Restaurant is in the Moorish style, the look that the Arabic and Berber people brought to Spain long before P&O first sailed there. The inspiration for the Alexandria Restaurant comes from ancient Egypt. The architects have borrowed brilliant colours and shapes from the past to make sophisticated rooms for today and tomorrow.

Dinner is always a special occasion on a P&O cruise ship. The two main restaurants aboard *Aurora* are designed to make every meal exceptional because there are always some occasions when you want a bit more formality at lunch, or you would like to be served at breakfast or teatime.

Everything is comfortable, stylish and welcoming, though your surroundings are distinctly grand. You will be greeted by a smiling waiter who already knows you and what you particularly like. New and old friends will be at the same table. The menu describes mouthwatering world-class dishes. Enjoy your meal! How could you not?

The same experienced care goes into every detail of your dining experience aboard *Aurora*. The waiters fuss over the glittering cutlery, plates and glasses. The table linen is perfect. Even the dining chairs – made specially for the Medina Restaurant – were worried over for months by the design team. They must be stable, comfortable, durable, handsome. The menu cards feature ‘Ships of P&O 1866-1937’. None was so carefully planned, none so beautifully run as *Aurora*.

California Merlot

Britons drink more wine today than ever before and *Aurora*'s stylish younger passengers keep up with the trend. The 14 wine stewards serve over 6,500 bottles of still wine on a typical 14-day cruise. The wine list is skilfully planned to provide a bottle that is right for everyone, for every occasion (not just gala nights) and for every dish; the knowledgeable stewards are particularly pleased when passengers ask for their advice.

Towards the end of each cruise, proud and happy, smiling chefs parade from the galley into the restaurants to receive the well-deserved applause of the passengers.

Tonight is the night of the traditional Black and White Ball. At the Executive Purser's table, the gentlemen in dinner jackets or white tuxedos and their ladies in black or white dresses look much as P&O's first class passengers would have looked in the 1930s at dinner on *Viceroy of India* or one of the 'Straths'.

Today is someone's birthday and another long-standing P&O tradition brings the smiling restaurant stewards around the table to sing their good wishes.

Formal dining is one of the things which P&O has always done best. What has changed over the decades is the quality of the food. Today it has a lightness and sophistication which would have surprised and delighted pre-war passengers.

The Company first sailed to India in 1842 and its Victorian passengers loved good curries; the Lascar seamen (as the Asian crew were then called) longed for their home cooking too. So the standard of Indian cuisine on P&O ships has always been exceptional. Today, *Aurora*'s Indian and Goanese stewards put on their traditional dress, the Orangery is specially decorated with Indian motifs for the evening, and in the galley Asian cooks grind and blend the spices for a mouthwatering Indian buffet dinner.

Café Bordeaux, the continental bistro-style restaurant on Devanha deck (8), is open 24 hours a day. It provides the choice and flexibility today's passengers want. Because there is so much to do aboard *Aurora*, many people will choose to eat earlier or later than is possible in the formal Medina and Alexandria restaurants. If they feel like a Croque-Monsieur at four in the morning, this is the place to come to. The menu in Café Bordeaux changes according to the time of day or night. So you might have a pastry and Mocha for breakfast, a light lunch of Grilled Blackened Swordfish Steak on a bed of Niçoise Salad, and a Entrecôte de Boeuf with Five Peppercorn Sauce and Pont Neuf Potatoes for supper.

The sweeping circular stairway, handsomely panelled in a chequer-board of polished woods, leads up to the Café Bordeaux from Champions and the Monte Carlo Club casino on the deck below. Players can conveniently relinquish the hazards of the roulette table for the calmer pleasures of the café tables, or vice-versa.

Music ar

d Laughter

Crow's Nest
With the ship's best views, a stylish cocktail bar and music for dancing in the evening, this is a perfect place from which to watch the world float by.

Curzon Theatre
There are 660 seats in the theatre, but they are quickly filled. Singers and dancers love the Curzon too, because the revolving stage and state-of-the-art lighting and sound equipment give every performance a West End glitter.

Anderson's
Sitting at the long bar or in front of the fireplace in Anderson's, you could be in an exclusive country club. The traditional sofas, deep armchairs, bookcases and panelled walls have a very English feel about them.

Charlie's Champagne Bar
The ceiling in Charlie's is adorned with tiny rock-crystal lens heads which create a glittering starry effect. Champagne sparkles in the glasses too, and a cool pianist adds a note (or two) of gaiety and celebration. A place to relax and a place to be seen.

Masquerade
An ultra-modern night club and bar where the latest sounds test the state-of-the-art equipment to the limit until late, late at night. A video wall, stunning light effects and futuristic decor make Masquerade the glitziest club afloat. Very current, quite exhausting, brilliant.

The Playhouse
Aurora's second theatre, the 213-seat Playhouse, screens films so new that they have yet to reach your local cinema and is the venue for port enhancement talks, lectures and classical recitals.

Champions
A genuine sports bar where you can enjoy a beer or a short while watching major sporting events, both live and recorded, on big-screen TV. Or you can take your refreshment outside onto the Promenade deck and cheer on your friends as they stride around the ship. The bar is full of memorabilia of great sports moments and personalities.

Pennant Bar
An island bar overlooking the stern terraces. The centre of many lunchtime activities during the day and a good place to sit watching the wake stretching away as evening approaches.

Carmen's
Aurora's other main entertainment arena, Carmen's has a retractable stage, dancefloor and full service bar. You get a wonderful view of the stage from anywhere in the room and the shows are fantastic.

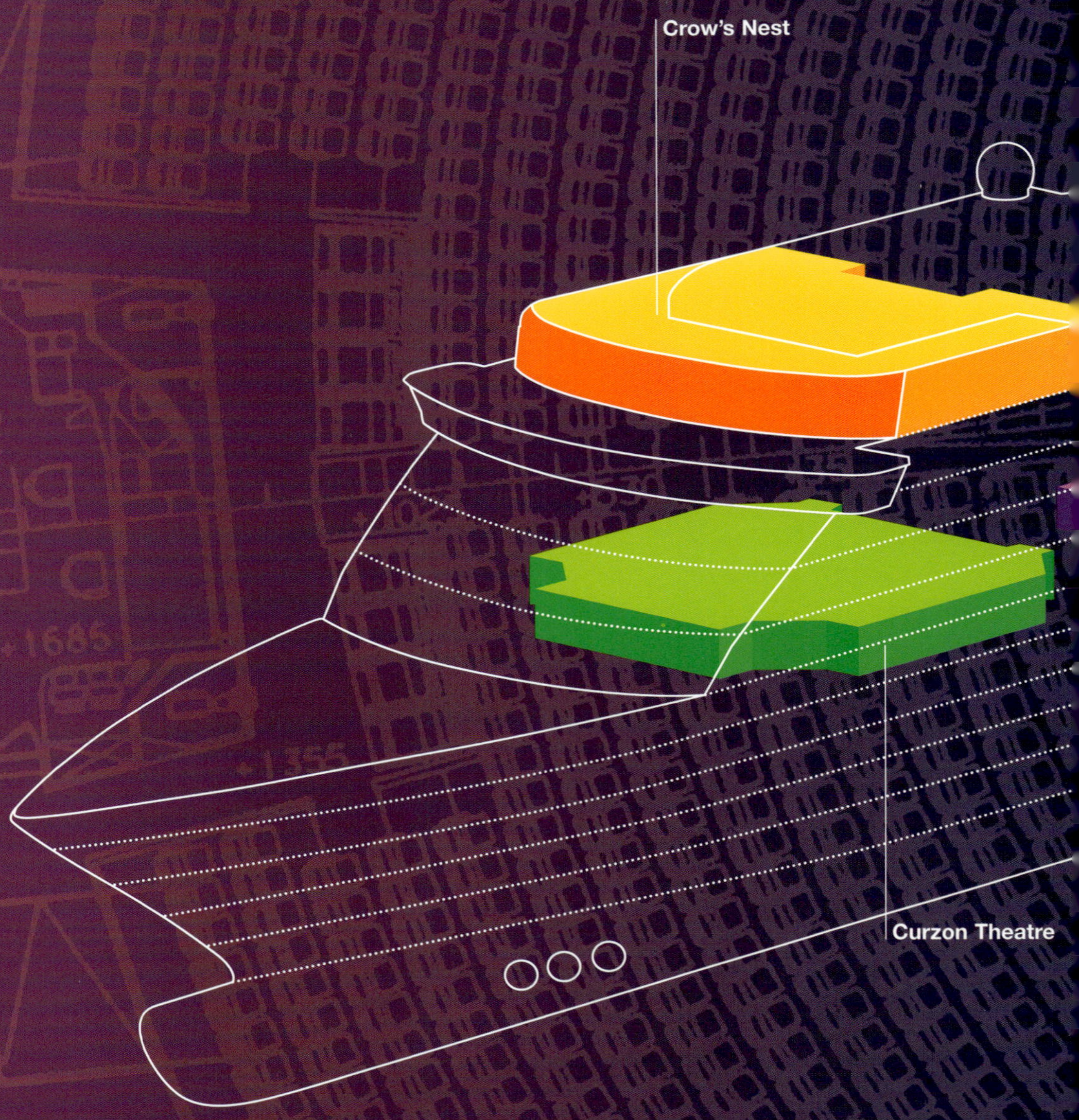

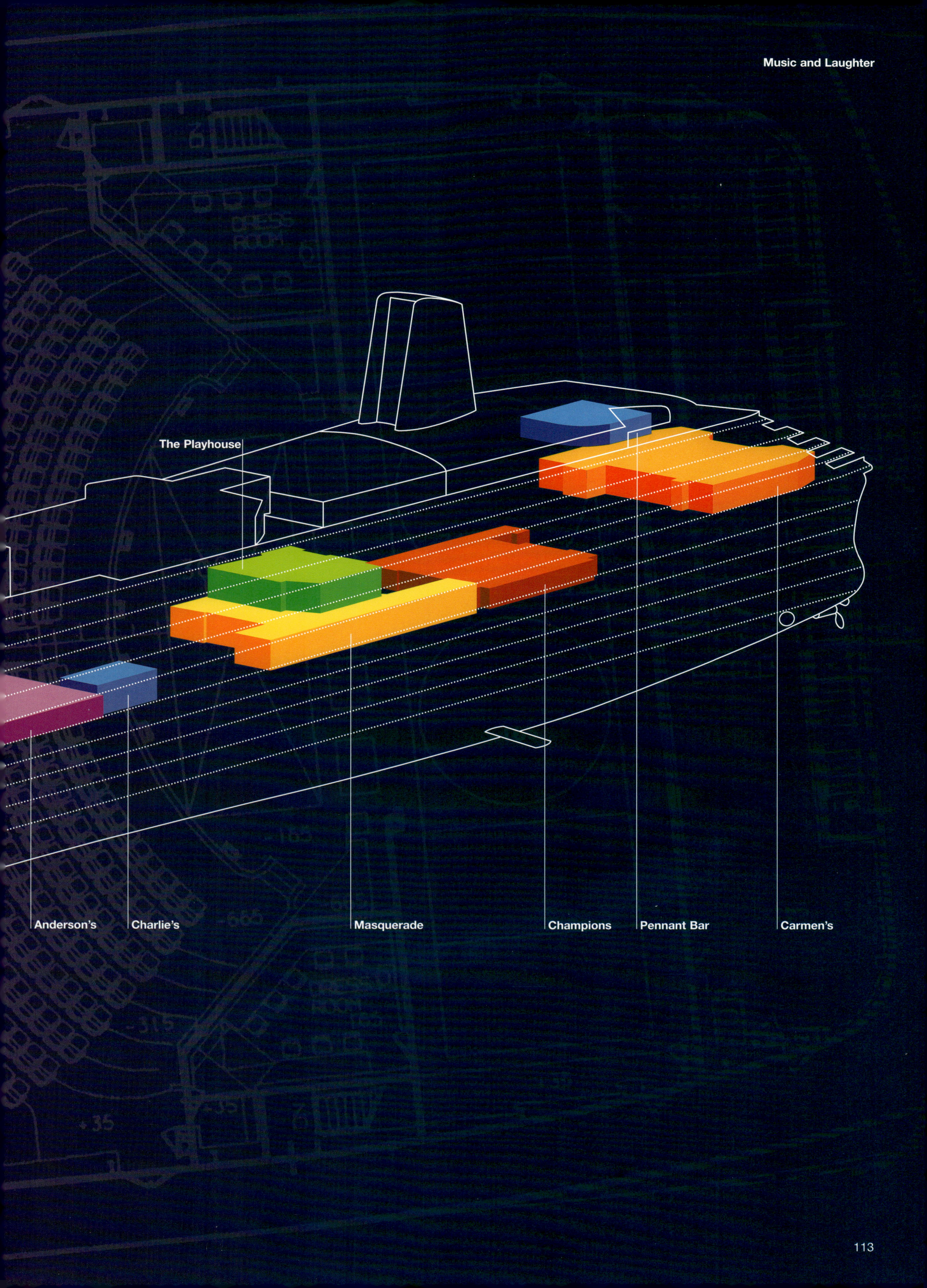
The Playhouse
Anderson's
Charlie's
Masquerade
Champions
Pennant Bar
Carmen's

Phil Raymond, *Aurora*'s Cruise Director, is a real trouper. He first appeared on stage at the age of seven and has toured the club circuit in the north-east, so he knows a great variety theatre when he sees one. The Curzon Theatre has every technical advantage a performer could wish for and what is so unusual on a ship, it has space. The stage is 24 metres (79 ft.) across; wonderful for the dancers, a blessing for the stage hands. There is a fly-loft above it into which the scenery can 'disappear'. The dressing rooms have space for the hundreds of costumes needed for the shows. The orchestra pit rises at the touch of a button, adding a wide fore-stage to the main performance area if needed. And there are two motorised stage 'revolves' (like at the London Palladium) to add impact to the variety.

Chris Blackburn, Technical Manager, is responsible for making it all work perfectly. In the control room he rehearses complex sound and lighting effects.

A craftsman applies the gilding to a column in the auditorium, the real gold leaf which adds richness to the Curzon Theatre's traditional theatrical colour scheme of red plush, maroon, and blue.

Two dancers in the wings of the 660-seat Curzon Theatre. The show tonight is *Oscar* and it's a full house. There are two performances every night and a different show every day. The girls have joined P&O's Stadium Theatre Company for the summer season. Last year they were both in West End musicals.

You have woken early and come up to the Crow's Nest, hoping to see land ahead. Higher than the bridge, you will be the first to see it. Enjoy the silence. By evening *Aurora* will have arrived, and the Crow's Nest will be packed with people enjoying the music and the best view aboard.

The crow's-nest was a barrel or box fixed high on the mast of a whaling ship in the days of sail to give protection to the look-out man. Things have improved since then. Sitting in the Crow's Nest lounge bar, *Aurora*'s passengers look out from a height of about 32 metres (105 ft.) above the water and can enjoy a drink without seeing the decorative cherry blow away. But they will still see dolphins playing in the bow wave, and the occasional whale.

Arthur Anderson (1792-1868) was a Shetlander who started work when he was only 11 years old and who became the Chairman of P&O. He believed in leaving his desk in the City and regularly going on the company's ships to ask passengers what improvements they would like made. He fussed over details until things were done perfectly – still the P&O way. Anderson would have enjoyed a malt in the comfortable Victorian surroundings of the bar that keeps his name alive.

In Carmen's, the singers rock through 'We Are The Champions' from *Queen By Appointment*, a tribute to Freddie Mercury. It is one of the most popular shows the company does. It's loud and young and outrageous – in the nicest possible way. When the show is over the audience will take over the dance floor and the music will cool down a little.

Two glasses of champagne in Charlie's bar and the pianist quietly playing 'our tune' rewaken romantic memories. There is nowhere better for two people to spend a quiet moment together at the beginning or at the end of an evening.

On an average 14 day cruise, *Aurora* gets through 2,500 bottles of spirits and 250 bottles of liqueurs. Who can resist the Cocktail of the Day – in this case the Margarita? The salty rim to the glass, the tequila, Cointreau and limes take you in one sip from Southampton Water to Acapulco.

At the Captain's Reception Party, the mood is cheerful. Captain Burgoine has a friendly word for everyone.

TEACHER'S
DRY SACK

What an evening! The photograph will provide a long-treasured reminder of that gala night aboard *Aurora*. They both felt so young again. It began with the formal dinner in the Medina Restaurant with dear friends and they all drank to the next time and promised to come again. Then they went to Masquerade and he teased her until she agreed to dance ('though the other couples were half our age', she says), then, feeling lucky, a modest flutter at the roulette table in Monte Carlo. And just when he thought they ought to be going to bed, she said 'why not let's have a quick cup of coffee and talk over the evening in Raffles?' So they did. The coffee had a dash of something in it and the chocolates were so good she couldn't manage more than two.

Dancing beneath the stars on the deck of a great ship, set in a deep blue sea. An exciting shore, dimly visible, promised for tomorrow. A buffet of tempting dishes. Live music. Lovely people. Evenings don't get much better than this.

This is *Aurora*.

Figure it Out

Ship Shape
Length overall: 270 metres (886 ft.)
Gross tonnage: 76,000 tons (this is a measure of *Aurora*'s internal carrying capacity, her volume, not her mass or weight)
Cost to build: £200 million
Area of ship's side: 10,000 sq. metres (three times the area of the sails of *Cutty Sark*)
Open deck space: 9,200 sq. metres (equal to more than 35 tennis courts)

Building Blocks
Weight of steel used in construction: 20,000 tonnes
Engines produce 58,800kW = enough electricity for York
Propellers turn at up to 142 revolutions per minute
Best turning circle (without thrusters): 463 metres = ¼ nautical mile (at 16 kts)
Fuel oil burned between Southampton and Gibraltar: 435 tonnes (43,500 litres)
White paint needed to paint the ship: 100,000 litres (21,997 gal)
Total amount of cabling on board: 2,000 km
Axminster carpet fitted: 50,000 sq. metres

Voyages
Best speed: 24 knots = 27.6 mph or 44.4 kph
Distance sailed in a typical year: 83,000 nautical miles
Number of ports visited in 2000: 64 on 18 cruises
Fuel oil burned between Southampton and Gibraltar: 435 tonnes (43,500 litres)
Distance to the horizon from the Crow's Nest: more than 13 nautical miles

On Board
Number of passengers (normal): 1,850
Passenger decks: 10
Passenger cabins: 934
- 2 two-deck penthouse suites
- 10 suites with balconies
- 18 mini-suites with balconies
- 96 staterooms with balconies
- 272 twin cabins with balconies
- 225 outside twin cabins
- 16 outside family cabins
- 273 inside twin cabins
- 22 disabled cabins

Chairs on board: 6,200 (excluding stools and sofas)
Cakes eaten on a 14-day cruise: 42,000
Number of teacups on board: 8,736
Ice-cream eaten on a 14 day cruise: 4,000 litres (nearly enough to fill 35 bath tubs)
Champagne consumed in a year: about 13,000 bottles

Acknowledgements
Theo Hodges and Garry Pownall would like to acknowledge the help of those at P&O Cruises, particularly the New Build, Technical, Hotel Services, Operations and Marketing departments. Jim Hunter, John Cowe and the Project team, Bernard Meyer and the team at Meyer Werft, Captain Burgoine and his officers and crew, P&O Aviation, Stephen Rabson, and the passengers and crew of *Oriana* who helped with the shoot.

Additional Photography: Jason Hawkes, Norman Brand, Ingrid Fiebak. The publishers are grateful to the following for permission to reproduce photographs: Comstock, Telegraph Colour Library, TCL Stock Directory, Science Photo Library.

Some of the more generic cruising shots were taken on board *Oriana*, *Aurora*'s sister ship.

Printed by The Beacon Press, UK.
Design & production of *Aurora – Dawn of a New Era* by Theo Hodges Business Design Consultants, telephone: 020 7351 0749.

Published in Great Britain by P&O Cruises (UK), Limited
77 New Oxford Street, London WC1A 1PP

The Peninsular and Oriental Steam Navigation Company
ISBN 0-9514328-2-6